Penguin Handb

POTS AND P

Gertrude Harris is a graduate of New York University and has served as director of several galleries of contemporary art in New York City, Monterey, California and Rome. She has contributed art reviews and criticism to a number of periodicals and European newspapers, and her poetry has been represented in several anthologies. She is also the author of *Manna: Foods of the Frontier* and *Pasta International*.

Gertrude Harris developed an appreciation of fine food and unusual cookware in the New York home of her Russian-born parents, who instilled in her the philosophy that quality in food, as in all things, is more vital than quantity. Her serious interest in cooking and cookware, however, started with her marriage to the painter-sculptor Zev, a 'great gourmet and serious cook'. In her early married years in New York City and later during the eleven years they lived in Europe, she passionately collected unusual, exotic and old cooking implements; then set about learning how to care for them and use them properly.

Roy Killeen is a San Francisco architect turned publisher. A graduate of Washington University, St Louis, he was an associate of William B. Ittner, Inc., St Louis, and project architect for Anshen and Allen, San Francisco, before founding the publishing company of 101 Productions. In addition to serving as president and art director, he has illustrated a number of 101 books – *Soup*, *101 Secrets of California Chefs*, *101 Nights in California* and *Country Inns of the Far West*. He also designs a series of architectural kits for 101.

GERTRUDE HARRIS

POTS AND PANS

Preface by M. F. K. Fisher
Illustrated by Roy Killeen

PENGUIN BOOKS

Penguin Books Ltd, Harmondsworth, Middlesex, England
Penguin Books, 625 Madison Avenue,
New York, New York 10022, U.S.A.
Penguin Books Australia Ltd, Ringwood, Victoria, Australia
Penguin Books Canada Ltd, 2801 John Street, Markham,
Ontario, Canada L3R 1B4
Penguin Books (N.Z.) Ltd, 182–190 Wairau Road,
Auckland 10, New Zealand

First published in the U.S.A. by
101 Productions as *Pots & Pans Etc.* 1971
Revised edition 1975
First published in Great Britain, with revisions, by
Penguin Books 1980

Made and printed in Great Britain by
Richard Clay (The Chaucer Press) Ltd, Bungay, Suffolk
Set in Linotype Pilgrim

I dedicate this book with love to my husband, ZEV; with gratitude to Mary Frances Fisher and Elizabeth David for long hours of enjoyment and endless pages of inspiration; and to Mr Chuck Williams for generous help with this second edition.

Contents

Preface to the Second American Edition

It has often been told us, in one form or another, that it is easier to lie sometimes than to tell the truth. I have never found this so: I have been acutely miserable in my few attempts to prove the theory, and that is why I feel very comfortable in stating what is for me a plain fact about Gertrude Harris's little jewel of a book, *Pots and Pans*.

It is a jewel.

Thanks to it I now count the writer as a friend, but long before I had met her, and only shortly after I had read the book, I wrote her one of the two or three fan letters of my life, with sincere thanks for what she had done. That was about four years ago, I think. Now there is this new edition, and it is even more of a Kitchen Friend than the first one, if that be possible.

Near my stove there is a short shelf of books that are *needed*, any time of day or night, so *Pots and Pans* is always close to hand. I buy a new heavy-gauge aluminium saucepan (which I do every thirty years or so), or somebody gives me a cast-iron soup kettle for my Franklin stove (once in a lifetime!), or I decide to use stainless-steel spoons (which I did lately). I reach for my little paperback, and go ahead confidently with the new acquisitions. And all the time I wonder where else on God's green earth I could find such help, except in this book ...

The main trouble with it is, that after I have let it answer my current question, I go on reading what else Harris has to say on momentarily irrelevant subjects, except of course, that they are all about cooking tools. I smile, for instance, at her obvious aesthetic enjoyment of two large brass pans she bought, from Hong Kong: '... Although the metal is fairly thin, the rims of both pan and lid are cleverly worked into a beaded edge to give the pan sturdiness and solidity. The lid fits firmly into a "ditch" formed by the beaded edge, which also prevents condensed moisture from escaping down the sides of the pan. The design and handcraft ... triumph over the disadvantages of the thin metal.'

This description is eminently practical, but it reveals a kind of empathy with the subject of what St Teresa called her 'pots and pipkins' that subtly enlivens the whole straightforward treatise.

Nothing could be more candid than Harris's advice on the care and usage of materials. In the section on vitreous

enamel she writes of the latter, 'If food has stuck or burned on, soaking with a little soapy water, to which a little ammonia is added, should take care of it. If a roaster, used in high oven heats, has a stubborn stain or foods stuck to it, I sometimes spray on a little "window cleaner" (the kind with ammonia added) and leave it on for a while. It seems to do the trick.' The whole small book is unadorned by fancy language, but it has real style, and now and then a wry or subtle joke may be left dangling for the wary reader ... *only* if it will not mislead anyone, of course. And there is a continuing feeling that the author knows by both instinct and training what she discusses, as when she says casually, 'It is well known that a chef's knife, like a cowboy's pony, will not permit a stranger to ride it.'

And the research behind all this seemingly modest and casual guide to kitchenware is awesome, to my mind. There is the index, of course, an excellent one. And then there are chapters like the one about aluminium and its care, which also asks if it is 'safe'. (Choose your poison, as the old bartenders used to say ... but Harris is both fair and reassuring.)

At the risk of sounding either hired, which I am not, or moonstruck, which I have not been for several decades, I shall try to be as plain and sensible as the prose I am discussing, and make a flat statement that I think this book should be given to every child of ten if bright and of twelve if somewhat retarded. It should be kept on hand, straight through high school (chemistry classes, etc.: metals ... alloys ... acids ...) and on into inevitable connubial complications, many of which focus as much in the kitchen as in the bedroom. And once consulted ... the burned skillet, the new egg-poacher ... it will remain close by, neat in design and format, and clear in its wisdom.

It is indeed a jewel.

M. F. K. Fisher
1.11.74

Introduction

Nothing new under the sun? Think! Less than a hundred years ago aluminium and stainless-steel pans were completely unknown ... But what is not new is the idea that although it is perfectly possible to cook a meal, and a good one, with almost any kind of utensil in almost any condition on any type of heat (in a tin can over a campfire, for example), it is certainly easier, quicker and far more economical in the long run to do so with a wisely selected utensil, wisely used.

And what is a 'wisely selected utensil' for *your* purpose? Only *you* can know that. All I can do is spell out the relevant facts, list the 'bewares' and point out how each type can best be used and cared for, then it's up to you to weigh this information and arrive at a conclusion that is economical, labour-saving and, above all, pleasant for *you*.

I am delighted to have *Pots and Pans* re-issued by Penguin, London, whose editors have my blessings in deleting and rewording, where they deem necessary, the text, for English readers.

I never would have remembered that the cookware we call porcelain, or enamelware, you call vitreous ware. Nor that our aluminum is your aluminium. And I am well aware that even small differences like these may well make reading unpleasantly halting.

As some changes in cookware appeared between the first edition in 1971 and the second in 1975, I expected that I would have many more innovations to report in this, the third edition.

Though many manufacturers – in the United States and in some European countries – have *improved* their merchandise, I can find no basic or vital changes in material or even in design in the new kitchenware. More pans are heavier, better balanced, more substantial and with promise of longer life, thank goodness, for the higher prices now being asked – and paid. So the warnings in *Pots and Pans* need no changing.

The greatest difference is, it seems to me, in the cooks and the buyers of cookware, then and now. Owing to the world-wide cookery 'revolution', cooks are demanding better value – and know what to look for and what to reject. Bravo!

Gertrude Harris
Point Richmond, California
October, 1978

In the Beginning

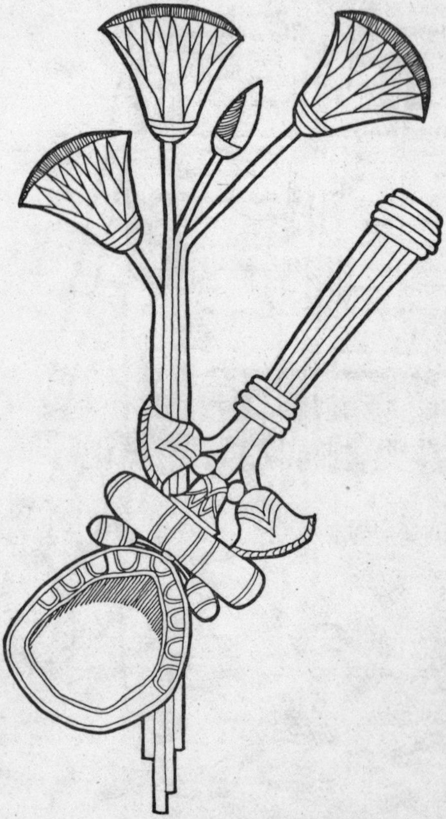

Cleopatra's Solution

There were, it is said, twelve kitchens in Cleopatra's palace in Alexandria. Each kitchen was an exact replica of all the others. Not only were they all the same size and furnished in precisely the same way, but there were exactly the same number of utensils in each kitchen. Naturally, all twelve presiding chefs held exactly the same status, chefwise, that is.

The compulsive foolishness of an absolute monarch? Not at all. She had good reason. Let's suppose Cleopatra had invited thirty guests to an intimate little soirée to honour a Major Poet. Hors d'œuvre were served, drinks were poured and the dinner hour, say, 8.30, was approaching. Cleopatra, turning to the poet beside her, praised an early poem of his. 'And what is your most recent work about?' she asked. The poet, flattered, thanked his queen and began a dissertation on poetry in her favourite genre. The minutes slipped by: 8.20, 8.30, 8.45. But one does not offend the muse.

Gentle reader, what would you have done had you been Cleopatra?

Well, this is how she worked it out: Kitchen 1 was prepared to serve dinner at 8.30 sharp. If that dinner could not be served, for the above reason or any other, then Kitchen 2 was to have the same meal ready to serve fifteen minutes later, at 8.45; Kitchen 3 at 9.00; Kitchen 4 at 9.15; and so on.

The Major Poet finally concluded his oration at 9.20. His appreciative audience, the perfumed oil from their head-cones smartly dripping down faces on to applauding hands, surreptitiously noted that the attendant page, peering from the doorway leading to the kitchen wing, had signalled to the sous-chef waiting at the door to Kitchen 5.

Cups were refilled with honeyed wine, the tray of Ibis Tongues aux Aten were passed for the last time and the first dinner course appeared promptly at 9.36.

And what happened to all the other complete dinners? My informant tells me they were tossed to the jackals!

I have often mulled over this curious bit of gastronomic history and my questions flow like Cleo's honeyed wine. Who bought all the kitchen equipment: the mistress of the house? Unlikely. True, most chefs owned their own tools, as they do even today, for it is well known that a chef's knife, like a cowboy's pony, will not permit a stranger to ride it.

First of all, the master chefs were hired and asked for a list of their needs. Architects built on the wing to house the twelve kitchens, and the finest craftsmen in the land were called to the palace and ordered to create the pots, pans, etc.

Surely the Queen wanted the last word: 'Make them the finest,' she ordered, 'the most beautiful and of the best materials obtainable. Mind you, they must be durable, for we will live forever; and they are not to fall apart in the first heat, so to speak ...' The artisans laughed obediently at the royal jest.

When the Queen had left, the chefs had the *very* last word: 'Hear this, craftsmen, if they do not please *us*, you will pay with your heads.' (How often have you wanted to use just that line on an appliance salesman?)

Apparently the kitchens and all the equipment were completed on the date set, and wonderful savoury aromas issued from those twelve hot, steamy rooms, those fragrant laboratories, that wing of the palace so like a matrix, a womb, in which the marvellous germinates, develops and emerges fullborn in flawless form.

For this relevant bit of historical research, I offer acknowledgement and thanks to the American artist, ZEV, resident in Rome, MCMLXXI.

Magic in the Modern Kitchen

The wealth of curious and obscure lore related to the materials and shapes of household objects has been traced back to the very beginnings of time, and many ancient superstitions influence us even today, particularly those associated with iron and salt.

Have you ever been in a gleaming modern kitchen when the cook spilled some salt? Did she stop everything, pick up a bit of the salt and throw it over her left shoulder as she mumbled a wish? You were witnessing a superstitious rite as primitive as an old witch's spell over the black iron cauldron at a black mass.

Until very recently in rural areas of the U.S.A. it was the custom to put a piece of iron and some salt at the foot of the cradle of a newly born child. And many early books advise the use of salt to clean iron cooking vessels (though we do not).

The most familiar of all superstitions, I suppose, is the practice of hanging an iron horseshoe over a threshold. It's lucky, but why? It represents three vital factors that defeated the witch's evil: it had the horned shape sacred to the Mother Goddess (the moon); it was an attribute of the sacred horse; and it was made of iron, the sovereign metal.

The iron cauldron had a curious double symbolism. It served as a matriarchal symbol of home, food and warmth, hanging over the fire, which was also a sacred symbol. Later the cauldron figured prominently in the concept of the witch, the black mass and the devil dances. Even there it served both evil and good, for in it was first cooked the magical liquid required for practising their evil ritual. Then the cauldron was refilled and the 'sabbat' meal was cooked to feed the entire group. It is said that salt was never served at these rites, for these were pastoral people and the use of salt was associated only with settled or agricultural people.

This reverence for iron has been traced to the ancestors of the 'little people', the early Neolithic and Palaeolithic

inhabitants of north-western Europe, who terrorized Europe well into the eighteenth and seventeenth centuries B.C. Shepherds and cattlemen, they were just barely agricultural; pastoral but not nomad; a small, dark, quick-moving people. When the fierce Iron Age Celts moved northwards, invading their territories and homes, only those who lived in remote areas escaped the massacre; they learned to fear and loathe the new metal, the agricultural skill and the iron bells of their conquerors. Their own skill with stone and bronze could not compete; iron was so much more abundant and those who used it so much more adept and ruthless.

The 'little people' found that their best defence was cunning and witchcraft. A sort of guerrilla warfare developed that struck equal terror, but of a different kind, into the hearts of the invaders. This was the beginning of the traditional fear of magic, and the superstition of the efficacy of iron and salt to baffle witches and fairies became a firm belief.

How to Buy Wisely*

Never before in our history has there been such a quantity of easily available consumer goods on the market, particularly cooking aids – in volume, variety, price and means of buying. The quality is so diverse and the quantity so vast that even the most experienced and astute purchasers need a mixture of talents to make the best buys, taking into account value for money, fitness for purpose and safety in use.

Newly-weds setting up home, or the experienced cook wanting to replace a battered old wedding present, need to understand something of the properties of the materials

*This chapter was rewritten by John Braun, consultant in consumer and European affairs.

used in the manufacture of kitchen utensils: glass and its variants, terracotta and other types of ceramics, vitreous enamel, plastics, metals and their alloys, as well as the processes of construction. They should, too, be aware of the chemical effects, if any, upon the foods they will cook in them and the effects, if any, of foods on the utensils.

How can one save money, conserve energy and time in the kitchen? How can one get good value? How is the consumer to know what is sales promotion and what is fact? A few simple warnings and rules are relevant (others appear in their proper place):

Buy in a reputable shop or from an established mail-order firm.

Buy goods made by reliable manufacturers.

Be wary of goods that are not backed by proper guarantees and be sure that you understand the terms.

Do not buy from doorstep salesmen unless you know who they are, whom they represent and precisely what they are selling.

Do not sign a contract without talking it over with someone who has experience in such things.

It pays to shop around and compare prices, especially when buying highly priced items.

Beware of slick demonstrations. If a contrivance is demonstrated to you, insist on trying it out yourself before buying. Such demonstrators are well-trained, and have been chosen for their ability to talk fast and move quickly.

Do not be afraid to ask questions until you are really satisfied.

Read carefully all labels, tags and manufacturers' leaflets.

Question the value of expensive kitchen and cookery ware sold in sets, often accompanied by 'free gift' offers. They may seem like fabulous bargains but the actual cost may be well above that of buying each piece separately.

Be careful at sales!

Have a budget: know what you need and want.

Where to Buy

Shopping takes up a great deal of time and the choice of shop is therefore important. The advice given earlier to buy in reputable shops should not be taken lightly. The shop may be an old-established hardware, china or general shop; a chain, multiple or department store; a specialist boutique-type shop or a supermarket with a 'pots and pans' section. Each of such shops may have varied advantages such as a delivery service, an advisory service on kitchen planning, a complaints procedure and easy exchange facilities. As a rule, most of these shops stock branded goods and when an article is at fault the reliable shop will exchange it and give you an immediate replacement, itself sorting out the problem of the defective article with the manufacturer. The reputation of good stores is based on good customer relations.

Discount stores or warehouses have the advantage of price but there is no delivery service, little or no expert advice and fewer facilities for complaining if things go wrong. Much equipment is sold already packed in cartons, choice being made from display samples. There is little chance to examine the actual item you are going to buy and it is advisable when you buy from such stores to undo the carton when you have paid for it and check the goods before leaving. This applies wherever you buy. Any unwrapped purchase should be opened and tested before it is taken away. With the best will in the world, the salesperson or retailer cannot know that an article still unwrapped is in perfect working order.

There has been a great expansion in mail-order business and selling in the home and care should be taken to deal only with reputable firms, preferably those recommended by satisfied friends and neighbours. Mail order is usually by catalogue and a choice can be made at leisure from a range of nationally branded goods. All good companies will exchange goods which do not give satisfaction. Direct selling by established firms has the advantage of in-home demonstration and if high pressure salesmanship occurs, it can be met by insistence on a cooling-off period to consider the purchase, and a return of the goods if you are not satisfied.

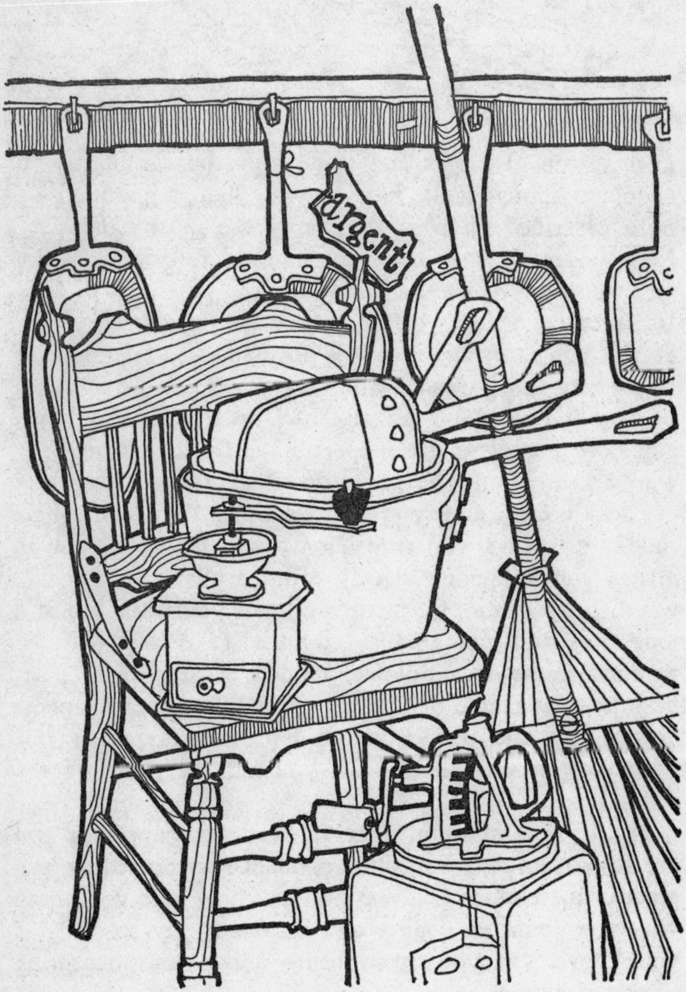

Shopping Around

Comparison of prices and value is an important part of shopping, though it can be overdone. 'Shopping around' has been described as 'possibly one of the most exhausting, time-consuming and mind-numbing of human activities' and whether you shop around for daily purchases of food, for instance, depends on the amount of time, strength and energy you can spare. But it is possible to be selective and to prepare the ground for buying what you want at the price you can afford to pay. Mail-order, discount house and store catalogues give opportunities for immediate price comparison, often referring to the same branded articles.

Check quality and type of model so that you can equate price with value. You may not want to pay much for an article you will not use very often, while it is probably worth paying more for something that you want to last a long time and give frequent service. Take care with remainder items or out-of-date models because spare parts may be unavailable or difficult to find. Balance cheapness against after-sales service and settle for what is right in your particular circumstances – for yourself, for two or for a family.

Try, or at least seem, to be an educated shopper. If you are suspicious of a utensil or appliance advertised as 'top grade', 'finest of its kind' or 'first class', be sure you know why you doubt its quality and be able to say so. Only if you know, can you avoid being drawn into accepting second-rate items.

Labelling

Get into the habit of reading labels and information tags on all articles. It is useless for consumer bodies to press for more informative labelling if people do not take the trouble to read and learn. There is a growing range of information available about household equipment and it is worth making the effort to interpret it correctly, particularly as this kind of equipment gets much wear and can cause discomfort or be a distinct hazard. If more than one person will be handling and using the equipment, the labels should be compulsory reading for every user. Once read, put them where they can be easily found later for reference. Keep all tags and labels together.

Make sure that where goods are labelled, your particular purchase has the label or the tag on it. If it is missing or there is no leaflet giving directions for use, do not buy, or if you have made up your mind that it is just what you want, insist that the salesperson provide you with the missing material.

Look for the Kite Mark, the British Standards Institution sign to show that certain products or parts have met the relevant safety and quality standards. All manufacturers who have the right to use the mark are subject to factory inspection and sample tests are made to ensure that the quality is maintained. Go for electrical equipment which is BEAB (British Electrotechnical Approvals Board) approved under the scheme covering the safety of electrical goods such as kettles.

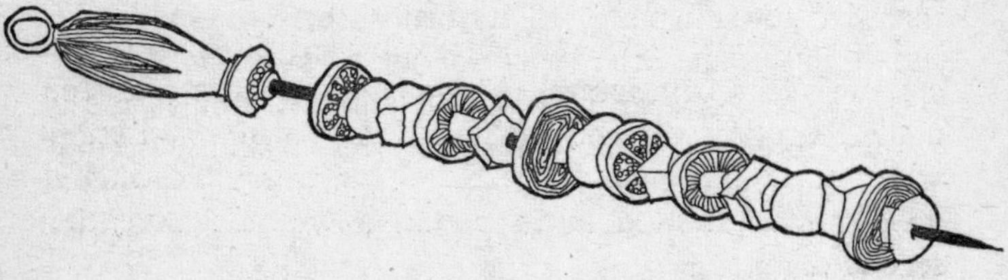

Consumer Rights and Guarantees

You should know that you have a number of rights under civil law which do not depend upon any guarantee. When you buy your pots and pans, or any other merchandise, you enter into a legally binding contract with the seller. You pay your money and, for his part, the shopkeeper warrants three things in particular (a duty conferred on him by the Sale of Goods Act as long ago as 1893). Firstly, the goods must be of merchantable quality, for example, a saucepan must have a firmly-fixed handle and a toaster must work when you plug it in. Secondly, the article must be fit for the purpose for which it is normally used, for instance, a kettle must not leak. Thirdly, the article must meet the description applied to it, so a saucepan described as made of copper must not be tin.

What are your rights if these conditions are not met? You are entitled to return the goods and ask for your money back. You may be satisfied with having the fault repaired or you may have the faulty article exchanged for a good one. Some traders may offer a credit note in exchange. Do not accept it. Insist on having your money back, as is your right. It is now a criminal offence to display a 'no refunds' notice in a shop or any other notice which purports to take away rights conferred on consumers by the sale of goods legislation.

Goods are frequently sold with guarantees, often made to look very imposing with a large heading in Gothic type. These guarantees are supplied by the manufacturer, not the retailer from whom you bought the goods, and therefore may give you some extra rights against the former although your rights against the latter cannot be taken away from you. The shopkeeper may well blame any fault on the manufacturer but it is the seller's responsibility to put things right. In the complicated technological age in which we live, it is usually necessary for faulty goods to be sent back to the manufacturer but it is not your job to do it.

However, it may be useful to have rights against a manufacturer, so where a guarantee provides for you to sign and post it off, do so. But read the guarantee carefully and see what you are being given and how long it is going to be valid.

Some manufacturers used to issue what purported to be a guarantee containing what are known as exemption clauses, for example, limiting the period of repair or replacement of a defective part. The object was to escape responsibility for negligence and the effect was to reduce the buyer's rights under the Sale of Goods Act. As a result of laws passed in 1973 and 1977, such clauses are now forbidden. Manufacturers' guarantees may give consumers additional remedies but must not take away any of their legal rights.

It is important to note that, as the law stands at present, the legal liability of the manufacturer is based on some negligence on his part during the manufacturing process, and that the consumer's rights against the manufacturer for damage or injury can be enforced only if the item is used by the purchaser according to directions and for the purpose for which it was intended. For example, if you used an aluminium pot to mix bleach or an acid and then, after insufficient cleaning, made a soup in it and can prove that the soup harmed you, because you used the vessel for a purpose for which it was not intended you cannot hold the manufacturer liable. Even if it was not specifically stated on the label that the pot should not be used for such a purpose, can you honestly state that a cooking utensil might possibly have been intended for any use beside cooking food?

All that has been stated above applies whether goods have been bought in a shop, from a catalogue, through a newspaper advertisement, from a doorstep seller or at a selling party in a private home. But the protection of the sale of goods legislation only extends to sales by traders, not private sellers, so keep a note of the names and addresses of the suppliers.

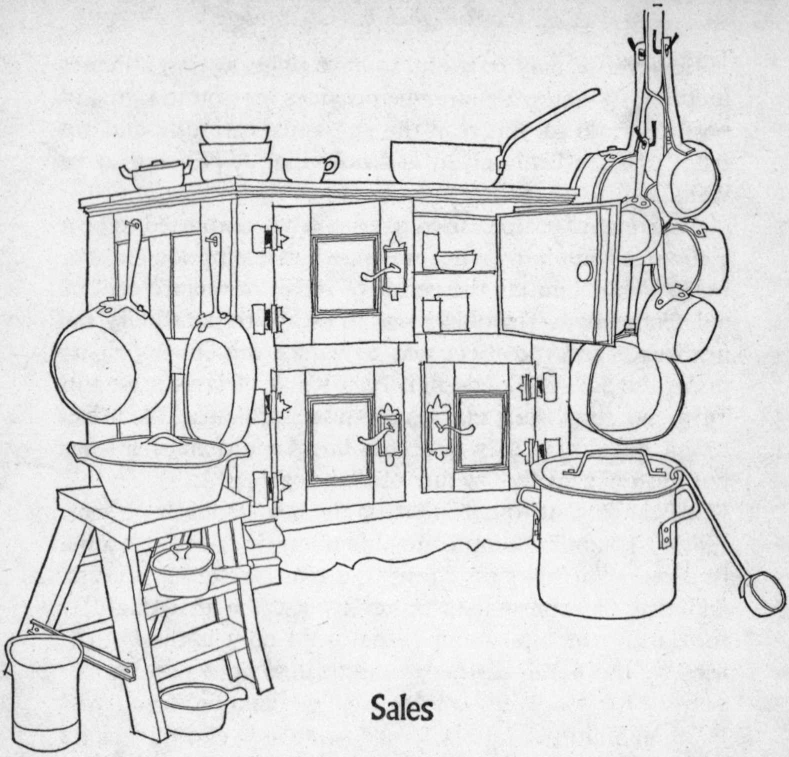

Sales

People who are very sensible in most matters of household affairs, often have one weakness – they cannot resist a sale or a 'bargain'. One such person has a box of items unneeded and unwanted and 'don't ever buy agains'. Now she gives them to church bazaars and charity jumble sales. As she says, 'I only give one or two at a time. I wouldn't want anyone to know how many I have.'

There is such a variety of types of special sales from 'clearance sale' to 'frustrated export sale' that you should maintain a healthy scepticism about all such descriptions. There are some shops where one kind or another of these sales seems to be taking place all through the year. Bargain offers, some very dubious, have become so prevalent that the law is constantly changing to keep abreast of malpractices. Trade descriptions generally are covered by the

Trade Descriptions Act of 1968 and there is a special section dealing with reduced prices. It is an offence to make a *false* claim of reduced prices at sales, such as 'Normal price £10 – our price £5'. Where it is claimed that goods have been reduced, it is assumed by the Act that the original price was charged by the trader unless the contrary is stated, and, unless a shorter period is stated, the goods must have been on sale at that price for a continuous period of not less than twenty-eight days during the preceding six months.

Some popular catchwords to note and understand about sales:

M.r.p. (manufacturer's recommended price), *r.r.p.* (recommended resale price) or similar phrases may refer to the usual selling price of the item. Manufacturers are forbidden by law to fix prices for retailers, hence the use of 'recommended' prices which may not always be based on a realistic figure so that retailers can appear to be giving a better bargain than they really are.

Clearance sale, at a reputable shop, may mean genuine price reductions on regular stock, often after stocktaking or to make room for new merchandise, particularly after Christmas and at the end of the summer. Such sales are also known as 'end of season' sales. Shop early to get the best bargains.

Special purchase may mean just that: merchandise purchased for that occasion to inspire some sales activity.

'Seconds' or *'imperfect'* are terms used to indicate substandard merchandise that does not come up to the normal level of quality control but is quite adequate for use. Chinaware is a fruitful source of bargains in this field owing to imperfections in throwing and glazing in pottery. Of course, these sale goods must still live up to the normal standard of merchantability and, although you must expect some imperfections, if the goods cannot be used, you are entitled to take them back.

How to Complain

It is never easy to complain about faulty goods because most people do not like making a fuss. But if articles are defective or do not do what was claimed for them, you are not asking a favour in demanding to have them put right.

When trouble arises, go first to the person who sold the goods, taking with you the bill, receipt, guarantee or any other proof of purchase you may have. In a small shop, ask for the proprietor; in a multiple or chain store, ask to see the manager. If you telephone, always ask the name of the person who deals with your query so as to pin down someone responsible.

If you do not get satisfaction in the form of one of the alternatives suggested in the earlier section on consumer rights and guarantees, seek some expert help from your local consumer advice centre or citizens advice bureau. Most often you will be helped through these agencies to have your troubles put right, but if not, and your purchase has been fairly expensive, you may have to sue the trader in the County court. Procedures are now much simpler, particularly for small claims, so going to court need not be too daunting an experience. If you are doubtful about the bona fides of the trader, or you are concerned about misleading descriptions or the safety of an appliance, you should go to the people responsible for protecting shoppers, namely the trading standards or consumer protection departments (the titles vary) of the local authorities.

Apart from legal remedies, some aspects of selling and marketing are dealt with by self-regulatory bodies, as for instance the following (whose addresses are given at the end of this chapter): the Advertising Standards Authority, for misleading advertising or sales promotion literature, posters and cinema advertising; the Independent Broadcasting Authority or the Independent Television Companies Association, for television or radio advertising; the Direct Sales and Services Association, for door-to-door and party plan selling; the Mail Order Traders Association of Great Britain, for mail-order catalogues; the Retail Trading-Standards Association, for descriptions and fair methods of retail selling.

For further and more detailed information as to how and where to complain, you should get the booklet *Fair Deal*, which is published, free of charge, by the Office of Fair Trading. It is obtainable at most public libraries and post offices or direct from the O.F.T. itself.

SOME OF THE LEGISLATION PROTECTING CONSUMERS

Sale of Goods Act 1893 and Supply of Goods (Implied Terms) Act 1973
Consumer Protection Act 1961
Weights and Measures Act 1963
Trading Stamps Act 1964
Misrepresentation Act 1967
Trade Descriptions Acts 1968 and 1972
Unsolicited Goods and Services Acts 1971 and 1975
Fair Trading Act 1973
Consumer Credit Act 1974
Consumer Transactions (Restrictions on Statements) Order 1976
Unfair Contract Terms Act 1977
Business Advertisements (Disclosure) Order 1977
Consumer Safety Act 1978

SOME USEFUL ADDRESSES

Office of Fair Trading: Field House, Bream's Buildings, London EC4A 1PR

National Consumer Council: 18 Queen Anne's Gate, London SW1

Consumers' Association: 14 Buckingham Street, London WC2N 6DS

National Federation of Consumer Groups: 70/76 Alcester Road South, Birmingham B14 7PT

Advertising Standards Authority: Brook House, Torrington Place, London WC1

Independent Broadcasting Authority: 70 Brompton Road, London SW3 1EY

Independent Television Companies Association: Knighton House, 52–56 Mortimer Street, London W1N 8AN

Direct Sales and Services Association: 47 Windsor Road, Slough, Berkshire SL2 3HT

Mail Order Traders Association of Great Britain: 507 Corn Exchange Building, Fenwick Street, Liverpool L2 7RA

Retail Trading-Standards Association: 360–366 Oxford Street, London W1N 0BT

The Kitchenware Primer

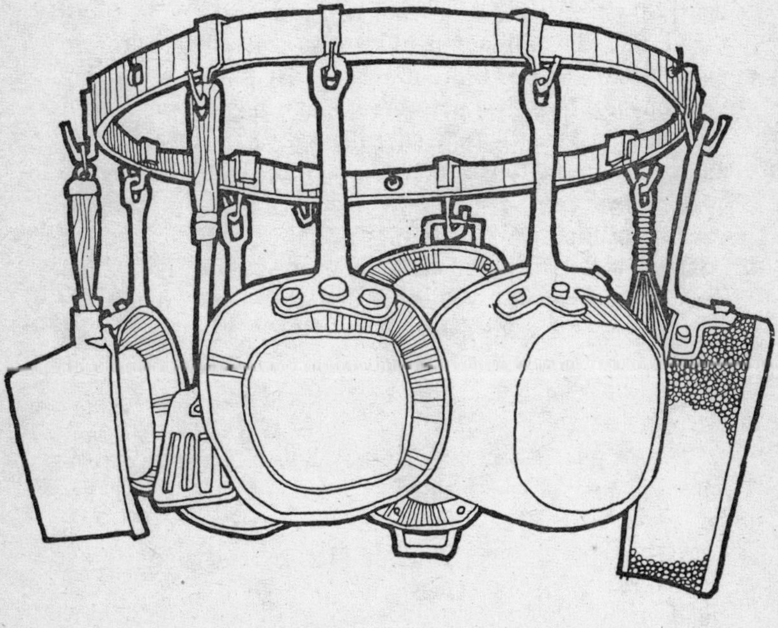

Materials: Care and Usage

A great cook can converse as intelligently about his tools and the materials of which they are made as he can about the recipes and the food for which he is famous. Awareness of the special properties of materials as well as the simpler methods of construction will directly influence judgement when purchasing, in care, handling and usage.

Even when a skillet or saucepan, pot or kettle, was made of only one material (iron perhaps, tin or even aluminium) such facts were important, but now that a pan may be composed of two or three different materials, it is essential. Innovations in kitchenware capitalize on the best features of each material and eliminate or minimize their limitations.

When all cooking was done over open fires, whether coal, wood or gas, and direct heat could reach every corner (or dent) of a pan, the form, condition and heat conductivity of the material was not significant to performance. On an electric burner, however, it is essential that the cooking vessel have a flat, level bottom (to make direct contact with the source of heat), be well balanced, in good condition and of a material that conducts heat quickly and evenly. In cooking over a gas flame, these factors simplify cooking as well as cleaning.

There is no one ideal material that suits all needs and does all jobs equally well; each has its advantages and disadvantages. It is expedient to have on hand a variety of kitchenware in a variety of materials chosen for particular types of jobs and adapted to the kind and quantity of cooking to be done.

For example, it would be shortsighted and indeed extravagant for an inexperienced cook to invest in a large, expensive set of diverse utensils all in the same material. Unless, of course, she has infinite storage space and doesn't mind duplicating and replacing utensils and implements as she develops her talents and tastes in the kitchen.

How then should the novice go about making a first purchase? Carefully! – and little by little, as he or she widens the range of activities. When we have discussed the characteristics of various forms of kitchenware and the materials in which they are obtainable, we will consider the best course of action in selecting the *batterie de cuisine*, which, roughly, translates into 'kitchen armament' or 'weapons of cookery'.

TYPES OF COOKWARE

What are the basic, the universal types of cookware and what are their distinguishing characteristics? A *saucepan* is a vessel with one handle. Some large saucepans have a movable carrying arm attached at each side, and some have two 'ear' handles or 'lugs'. A *skillet* or *frying-pan* is a shallow saucepan with a flat, relatively wide bottom. The sides may be sharply vertical, sloped, rounded or flared. Each type has many variations in size, shape, material and nomenclature.

All other considerations such as heat conductivity, balance, texture and price are determined by the material or combination of materials of which the utensil is made, the weight or amount of material involved, and the production methods used in making it.

And finally, different foods and methods of preparation demand different utensils. They will be used either *on top of the stove*, for boiling, frying, sautéing, stewing or pressure cooking; or *inside the oven* for baking, roasting or just warming; or *under the grill*.

Generally, materials meant for *surface cookery* are aluminium, stainless steel, iron, carbon steel, flame-proof glass, vitreous enamelware, copper, sterling silver, and flame-proof earthenware and china. Materials meant for use in the *oven* or under the *grill* are those used on the surface of the range as well as tinned steel or iron, soft earthenwares and heat-proof porcelains and china.

Lightweight materials heat very quickly and are desirable for short-term use (most often for baking) while heavier ones are more suited (and advisable) for foods that require longer cooking, for they heat more evenly and retain heat longer.

DISTRIBUTION OF HEAT

It should be clear by now that the most vital feature of a cooking utensil is its ability to distribute heat evenly. Pertinent materials graded from most to least efficient in this respect are: silver, copper, aluminium, cast iron, carbon steel, stainless steel, earthenware, porcelain and glass. The heavier the gauge (or thicker the pot), the more evenly the heat will be conducted. A vitreous-enamel coating will not alter this property in the base metal; a coating over thin steel does not change the fact that this pan will heat unevenly and rapidly.

In surface cookery, contact between utensil and source of heat is essential to make the necessary transfer of heat from source to pan to food.

Poor heat conductors distribute heat unevenly and erratically and, unless rigorously supervised, may cause what are called 'hot spots', points where food may stick and burn. This shortcoming is aggravated on an electric or thermostatically controlled burner, particularly if the bottom of the pan is not completely flat or if it is dented or warped and makes uneven contact with the heating element. Using low or medium heat can help somewhat to overcome this disadvantage. A perfectly flat bottom in any material will ensure better contact with the source of heat, avoid waste of fuel and cook food more evenly. An iron grid under a glass vessel will be helpful.

The heavier the gauge (or thicker the metal) of the pan, the more likely it is to resist denting and warping. The thinner the pan the more likely it is to warp, dent and heat so rapidly that the food is almost certain to burn unless great care is taken.

When cooking in water or with water (soups, stews, boiled or poached foods), the transference of heat through the liquid by its own currents (that is, by convective movement) will distribute heat smoothly despite poor conductivity in the utensil. But when cooking foods with high sugar or starch content, or during 'waterless' cooking, even heat conductivity is vital and the use of heavy aluminium, copper or cast iron is recommended to prevent rapid overheating.

For most purposes, cooking vessels with a dull finish (even shiny pots which are tarnished) are preferable to those with a shiny finish. Shiny materials *reflect* heat, rather than absorb it.

NEW MATERIALS

The larger cookware manufacturers have created new materials or blended the least efficient to the most efficient in ways that would have staggered the housewife only a few decades ago. We now take it entirely for granted that we can safely remove certain porcelain dishes from a freezer and put them directly into a preheated oven. Or that certain materials are now sandwiched between others or coated with a third or are so treated as to perform in hitherto unexpected ways, for more efficient usage.

Confusing to the layman is the manufacturer's practice of using different names for the same new materials or processes. This is perfectly legal. If even one tiny step during the production differs enough to warrant a separate patent, it is entitled to a new name. For example, many manufacturers are making utensils with a similar 'non-stick' coating on the inner surface of pans. The consumer must learn by experience that they all seem to serve the same purpose. For though the substances are not precisely alike (one may have some added element or be applied in a slightly different way; some are smoother, some rougher), they do *seem* to be the same, whatever they are called.

A familiarity with materials may make you seem knowledgeable on your next shopping spree, and that can be very handy, as every homemaker knows.

Virtually all materials intended for use with food are covered by legislation in this country and so, as long as you cook in a vessel designed to be used for the preparation of food, you should be quite safe. If you use something not intended for cooking you are taking more of a risk, so make sure you know what materials your food is coming in contact with. Articles that come into this category include vases, flower pots and plastic buckets or metal laundry pans (sometimes used for mixing large quantities of drink).

Silver

In a booth at the famous flea market in Clignancourt in Paris, I once found four silver saucepans of heavy gauge in graduated sizes. They had come, the dealer told me, from the kitchen of a 'princely house', and I could well believe it. In a long life of active coveting, I don't think I ever coveted anything more than those silver saucepans I simply could not afford to buy. Some time later I asked a friend, the proprietor of a renowned Paris restaurant, about them. His grandfather had two, he said; they had disappeared during the war. 'Ah *oui*, Madame, silver saucepans . . . ,' he mused. 'To make a sauce in a silver pan is never to forget it, like one's first ride in a Rolls Royce! The heat comes on so evenly – so evenly. And it comes rapidly to a boil, not here and there, but all over at the same time, and as one stirs, it is like making music, for the sauce thickens almost imperceptibly, gradually and just as it should, as one always hopes it will. And the flavour, Madame. It tastes only of the ingredients one has put into the silver saucepan. Do you understand? Just of the ingredients you want to taste, nothing else . . . *une cocotte d'argent* . . .' A long pause, and I remembered that a *cocotte* was many things besides a saucepan: a child, a little chicken, a darling, a sweetheart and a 'fast woman' – all these, and perhaps more. His tongue moved delicately over his lips, as did mine, I found. 'Copper, now, Madame. Well, copper is superb. A heavy copper pan is . . .' A Gallic shrug. 'Yes, copper is superb. Superb, Madame, but it is not silver.'

The reactions of serious cooks to mention of a silver saucepan are not too unlike the reaction of an archaeologist to mention of a wooden Mayan or Etruscan artifact; 'Amazing! Do they really exist?' Yet those same cooks often concoct their magic in silver chafing dishes. More often, I suppose, in silver plated over copper: the famous Sheffield formula.

Fine silver plate can be as expensive and valuable as sterling. The Sheffield formula was to plate heavy copper with fine sheet silver in three or four layers, making the silver heavy enough to withstand normal handling. The process, now improved, is used by many other firms all over the world.

Sterling silver is solid silver with 7½ per cent copper added for durability and hardness. Price depends on the maker, design and weight, or amount, of silver. Expensive, on the whole, but it should last for generations.

CARING FOR SILVER

To prevent tarnish, silver pieces should be wrapped in anti-tarnish cloth and stored in airtight chests or boxes or drawers. Do not use rubber bands against silver as they may contain sulphur and leave nasty marks.

Cleaning silver can be a long and tedious job or it can – like cleaning anything else – be quickly and simply done. Wash all silver as soon after using as possible. Do not soak. A few drops of ammonia added to the soapy water will cut through grease and add to the brightness. Silver knife handles are usually cemented to the steel blades and should never be washed in an electric dishwasher. Dry by hand, promptly.

For quick polishing, use a treated silver cloth. Dip-cleaners are not recommended for they may contain unsafe ingredients. There are a number of silver cleaners on the market, and you should follow the manufacturer's instructions. Goddard's Long Term is particularly good.

De-tarnishing baths are not for pieces with designs in high relief in which the crevices should remain dark. These baths are for fast, easy cleaning of smooth-surfaced pieces. Use a large aluminium pan, or an enamel pan with an aluminium rack or aluminium foil set on the bottom. Pour in enough water to cover the silver and for each quart (or litre) of water add one teaspoonful of baking soda. Bring the solution to a boil, then turn off heat. Add the silver and leave it to stand for a few minutes. Remove the silver, wash in hot soapy water, rinse and wipe dry. The aluminium sets up an electrolytic reaction with the silver sulphide and removes the tarnish.

The aluminium pan will have tarnished considerably as the sulphur from the silver deposited itself on the aluminium. Scour it with a soapy steel-wool pad or boil in it a solution of vinegar and water, or two teaspoonfuls of cream of tartar to each quart (or litre) of water. It will polish up almost as bright as new.

Copper and Brass

Copper casseroles, saucepans, kettles, *sautoirs, plats à gratin, marmites,* terrines, chafing dishes and crêpe Suzette pans are undoubtedly very elegant and look attractive on the dresser. But they are also wonderful to cook in, if heavy enough and handled with the care they merit.

Copper was one of the first metals to be used for cooking utensils and is, next to silver, the very best heat conductor. Two alloys of copper have also been widely used for cooking utensils: 'bell metal', with an addition of 20 per cent tin, and 'bronze', with 8 to 10 per cent tin. Cooking pots of both alloys have been dug up by archaeologists: some are almost as ancient as the history of civilized man. Bell metal was in use for cooking vessels as recently as the last century (mentioned in cookbooks and housekeeping manuals). Today both these alloys have few uses in the kitchen but many in industry and the arts.

PROS AND CONS OF COPPER

Copper utensils are extremely hard-wearing and were often handed down from mother to daughter as heirlooms, for a number of generations. In fact, I constantly use the copper pot my mother left me. It belonged to my great-grandmother and was brought to America by my grandmother in 1906. It has never yet been relined and is almost as perfect as the day it was made. The late Jean Varda, the Greek artist, was very amused to find that I had carried my copper pots when moving from Paris to London. 'Gertrude,' he sighed, 'you are like the old Greek women who, forced to flee from Cyprus to Turkey, carried only their copper pots and feather-coverlets.' Although hard-wearing, copper does dent easily, being a comparatively soft metal. The danger is minimized if the utensil is of really thick copper, as it should be. It is not a porous metal and will not pit, but it does tarnish upon exposure to air and heat. When in active

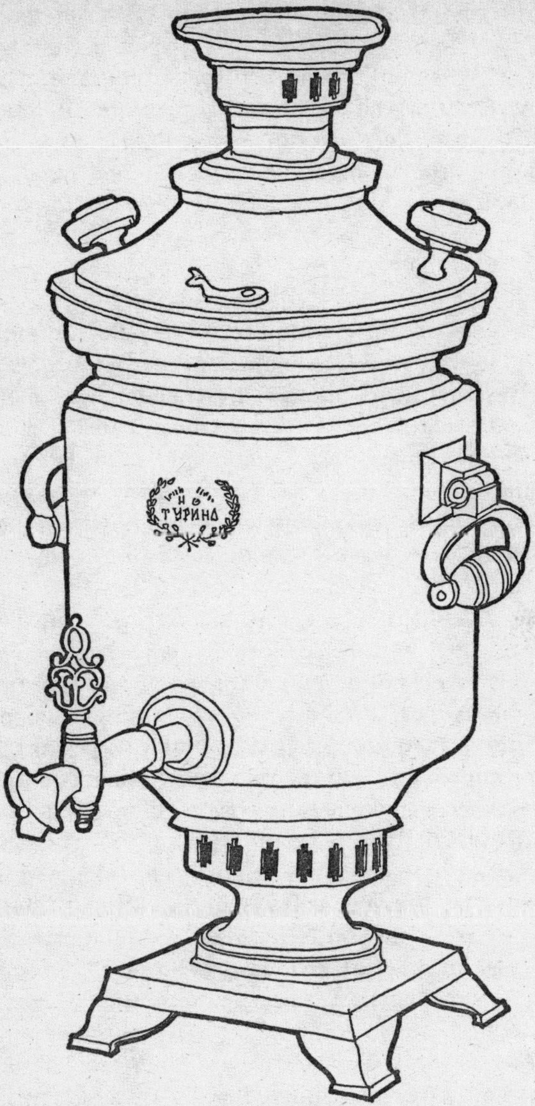
Н
ТУРИНА

contact with certain acids, unlined copper has an unpleasant taste and a distinct odour and will develop a growth called 'verdigris', a kind of green 'rust' that is poisonous. It is for these reasons that the interiors of copper utensils are plated or lined with silver or tin. Silver linings tarnish more quickly than tin but need less frequent renewal and, if possible, improve the heat-conducting qualities of the copper.

UNLINED COPPER

Several types of copperware are not lined. The traditional heavy half-globe bowl, in which egg whites are beaten, is superbly suited to its purpose. By chemical action the egg whites adhere to the bowl and whisk, causing air to be beaten in, resulting in larger volume (in any other material, the whites simply stick to the bowl). However, this miraculous action will work only if whisk and bowl are immaculately clean, so wipe both with cloth dipped in vinegar, before using.

Another unlined type is the heavy preserving pan for preparing foods with high sugar content: jams and jellies, etc. If this pan is not at least a 16th of an inch (or 1·5 mm) thick, you're wasting money! It should also be large (6 to 8 quarts or 7 to 10 litres, at least) and have a pouring lip (or two, for convenience and if you are left-handed). The pan is left unlined simply because the melting point of tin is lower than the boiling point of sugar.

A third type that is traditionally left unlined is the polenta kettle, described in detail in the section on 'exotica'.

Unlined pans should be cleaned as advised below in general cleaning, before and after each use.

COOKING IN COPPER

A copper pan worth its price, and the trouble entailed in keeping it clean and bright, is of a thick gauge, just as heavy as one can afford and can lift without breaking a wrist. As the price of copper has gone up so drastically since the end of the Second World War, fine copper utensils are as precious as jewels – or should be so considered and so treated.

Before buying or using a lined copper vessel, it should be absolutely and clearly understood that *never* – but never – must a metal tool be used in it for any reason whatsoever, because of the danger of scratching, bruising or otherwise removing the lining. Spoons, stirrers, forks, scrapers, etc. should be made of wood, hard rubber or plastic. If the food requires beating or whipping at a certain stage, remove it to another pan or bowl before doing so. And, unless you are very experienced and very, very careful, do not use your lined copper pans for sautéing or rapid browning of meat. The requisite degree of heat and lack of liquid will blister the lining. Never put an empty copper pan over heat, not even over low heat; be certain some food or liquid is in it. Rarely should copper pans be used over high heat; it simply is not necessary.

I submit that a thick copper pan is almost unequalled for long, slow cooking or for the blending of flavours in, say, the final stages of a fish stew or a *bœuf bourguignon*, a *pot au feu*, or as my mother used it, for the holiday *Gefulte* fish (and in thirty-five years it never burned, no matter how excruciatingly long was the emergency that tore her from the range).

One is always warned – and rightly so – not to store foods in copper even when the lining is perfectly intact. Since so much of our food is now being cooked in stages, to save time, such as making up a section of a complicated recipe some days before and quick-freezing it in the pot, I am constantly asked, 'But for such a short time, why not?'

Why not, indeed? I asked a Cordon Bleu graduate who teaches cookery and she told me she would not advise it at all. In fact, she *never* cooks a white sauce in copper or any other bare metal (whether or not it contains wine or lemon juice, the forbidden acid), for the metal may react and give off an unwanted flavour or colour. She recommends for that purpose the use of porcelain, enamel or glass. For a *roux*, a glaze or a brown sauce, copper is fine – but do not store (or freeze) it in the pan.

CLEANING COPPER VESSELS

Much new copperware leaves the factory with a protective coating of lacquer or plastic. If your piece is meant only to be decorative, this coating should not be removed. But if the piece is to be used over heat or for food preparation, it must be removed before use. The best way is to fill a large container with water and add one tablespoonful of washing soda for each quart (or litre) of water plus one for the pot. Bring to a rolling boil and immerse the copper piece in it for at least fifteen minutes. The lacquer or plastic should then just peel off. Wash as usual, rinse thoroughly and wipe dry. If your piece is very large, the coating may have to be removed with acetone, obtainable from a chemist.

The interior should never be cleaned with an abrasive or caustic material (scouring powder, among them) nor with a steel-wool pad. (Though, to my horror, I recently did come across such advice in a book by a very popular and indeed renowned authority. 'Clean,' she said, smugly, 'with a fine steel-wool pad.' It just makes no sense whatsoever.) If particles of burned food have stuck to the lining, pour in some warm water and set aside to soak *briefly*, then scrape with a nylon pad, a sponge or a brush; that should be sufficient. If not, whatever more you do, the pan will have to be relined anyway, so don't bother to scrub further. Let the 'plating man' do it for you. Never soak copper, iron or aluminium pots or permit food to stand in them – a sure way to ruin a fine pot. The exterior and handles of a copper pan can be cleaned with a commercial cleaner. The old-fashioned way suits me fine, however: dip half a lemon or lemon rind in table salt and rub over the entire surface, leave for a few minutes, then wash in hot soapy water, rinse very thoroughly and wipe dry promptly. Or, dip a sponge or soft cloth in a strong solution of salt and vinegar and proceed as with the lemon. Use this on unlined pots as well.

If the lining has worn or been scratched, the pan should be relined before being used again. However, if the lining is only very slightly scratched, the pan may still be used if it is cleaned with the vinegar-salt or lemon-salt mixtures *just* before it is used and the food removed from the pan immediately after cooking ... but it's risky.

RELINING COPPER

The question of relining copper pans can give some little trouble. A number of modern – and many old – cookbooks and housekeeping books suggest that copperware be *lined* (not plated) with *silver*, not tin. However, a few copper-plating people assure me that tin plating is as strong and durable as silver lining. 'Yes,' they say, 'there is some difference, but not much. The tin plating is an electrolytic process and the silver lining is "washed" on by hand; same price for each *process*, but silver costs half again as much as tin – and one wears as well as the other.'

Actually, there is a world of difference between electrolytic plating and what is called 'block tinning' or 'fire tinning', whether with silver or tin. The former results in a thin coating that wears off easily and quickly; the latter fuses the lining material to the copper, as both materials are red-hot during the process. It is called 'block tinning' because an actual block of tin is melted and applied. It is easily identified by rough uneven strokes, is shiny and wet looking. Yes, it is more expensive and few platers will bother now, but some still do. Firms that do relining of copper are found in the yellow pages of the telephone directory. Look under *tinners* and avoid like the plague those firms that boast of doing industrial or commercial work. Select those that are in small type or specify 'precious metals' and/or 'plating, polishing and repairing of silver, tin and copper'.

BUYING COPPERWARE

Now, if you are not yet put off copper and must have at least one piece, *do not do as I once did*: I am tempted by kitchenware as some women are by shoes (and, like Oscar Wilde's character, can resist everything except temptation). I bought, during a lean period, a thin Portuguese copper saucepan for it was so appealingly cheap. Using it as I do any other copper pan, it did not last long: a little under two weeks, I'd say. The sauce burned, the lining bubbled, the outside turned a funny pink, and it never did feel *real* in the hand. I should have bought shoes, instead.

At one time, most copperware came from France, but within the last few years, German, Swiss and Italian as well as British copper pans have appeared on the market. Examining them closely, one finds that even among the good, heavy ones, few are handmade anymore, though many are hand finished. One great danger in kitchenware of such weight is a lack of balance, so be sure to test them in the store, before buying. The French have a great respect, apparently, for this vital feature; theirs are rarely off balance.

BRASS

Brass is a copper alloy long used for cookware, though today rarely seen, except perhaps in Chinatown. When, some time ago, I found two large brass pans, I scooped them up. They were handmade in Hong Kong and look very much like Chinese porcelain bowls with handles. The lid is domed and has a saucer-like 'knob' for easy grasping. When the lid is reversed on a table, to act as a trivet under the pan, the 'knob' serves as a foot. The pans are made of sheet brass, hammered into form. Although the metal is fairly thin, the rims of both pan and lid are cleverly worked into a beaded edge to give the pan sturdiness and solidity. The lid fits firmly into a 'ditch' formed by the beaded edge, which also prevents condensed moisture from escaping down the sides of the pan. The design and handcraft of these pans triumph over the disadvantages of the thin metal.

Being an alloy of copper, brass has the same dangers as copper; so the pans are tin-lined.

Brass is certainly not a very commonplace material for kitchenware, but it is quite popular in the Orient, I understand. I enjoy mine thoroughly and use it much as I do copper, with a bit more care, since it is so thin.

Tinned Ware

The use of tinned kitchenware has been known since the 1600s. Dr Kitchiner in *The Kitchen Oracle* (1797) states: 'In small families we recommend block tin saucepans, etc. as lightest and safest. If proper care is taken of them and they are well dried after they are cleaned, they are by far the cheapest; the purchase of a new tin saucepan being little more than the expense of tinning a copper one ...'

The 'block tin' referred to is simply another name for the tinware we usually use for ovenware: a coating of tin over iron or steel. The more popular pieces of tinware are for cake tins, pie dishes, pudding moulds, bread tins, etc. When making suggestions for the *batterie de cuisine*, more detail will be given. *Tinned ware* is the accurate term since it is a base metal coated with tin, or 'tinned'. It is lightweight and graded according to the quality and thickness of the base metal (usually steel) and of the tin coating. The more heavily coated sheets are called 'block tin'. The heavier the coating and the better the quality of the tin, the more durable the vessel and, of course, the more expensive.

Food acids affect the tin. It tends to darken with use and age, but tarnish is a protective coating to the tin and improves its heat-absorbing qualities.

Tinned ware should not be scoured nor should abrasive cleaners be used on it, at the risk of scratching the coating and exposing the base steel which will rust and corrode rapidly should moisture reach it. Many of the fashionable French kitchen utensils are of tinned metal, and they are now easily available (albeit at prices that twist my heart and bring an upsurge of desire for travel!). One should know that they are best and most easily cleaned with nothing more complicated than old-fashioned cheap washing soda or baking soda. Sprinkle some on a cloth or sponge and rub over the tinned piece. Rinse well. Wipe dry promptly. To remove burned-on food, soak in a weak solution of baking soda or washing soda until food becomes soft enough to wipe off.

Iron

The first use of cast-iron vessels is said to have been in China for water kettles and rice bowls. During the Middle Ages in Europe, cast-iron utensils were listed in household inventories along with the family treasures. In colonial America, most of the basic necessities were of iron. Early cooking implements, hung around the fireplace, included such fascinating tools as trammels, gridirons, spits, jacks, pothooks, cranes, tongs, skillets, kettles, toasters, trivets, knives and spoons.

Much of the early ironware remained in use, unchanged, until well past 1820 and 1830, particularly in rural areas. Until well into the nineteenth century, iron was of a pale grey colour and housekeeping advisers suggested cleaning until the black disappeared and the grey emerged. Julia McNair Wright wrote in 1879 in her book *The Complete Home*: 'The practice of washing [iron] pots and pans in soiled dishwater, wiping them with a wrung out dishcloth, and hanging them up all black and shiny within, is dirty and unhealthful. Clean iron has a grey look.'

The cast-iron ware used today is greatly improved and made of alloys that give greater strength and permit thinner and lighter castings. Iron utensils are either cast into the desired shape or formed by pressure from sheets of high-carbon steel. They have many common properties that I will discuss separately.

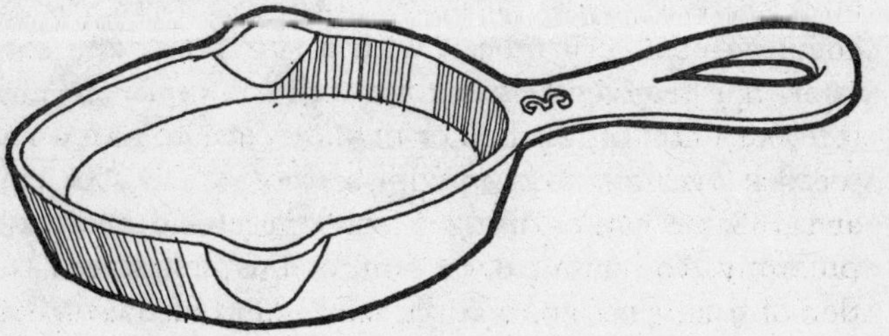

CAST-IRON WARE

Cast iron is used for many cooking utensils such as skillets and frying-pans, large casseroles, griddles, grill pans, muffin pans and such fascinating objects as the Scandinavian Plätt griddles, Munk pans and wafer irons. Apart from the familiar heavy black pot, cast iron is now available with rust-resistant finishes, fine vitreous-enamel coatings and non-stick linings. Pots with these finishes obviously require different treatment from unlined cast iron.

Cast iron is heavy, tough, hard but fairly brittle and may break upon severe impact or if dropped. Acids and alkalis may affect the metal and cause pitting.

Cast iron conducts heat evenly, retains heat well and can withstand most normal kitchen temperatures. It is especially valued for sautéing and browning foods. Cast iron is said to be the only common material to have both those desirable qualities of heat conduction and heat absorption, the latter because of its dark colour. Unfortunately, air and moisture quickly oxidize it, forming a red rust which in time could eat through it. As iron is a fairly porous metal, it is necessary to season it before use in order to fill the 'pores' with a coating of oil or *unsalted* fat. Although many utensils are now pre-seasoned at the factory before shipping, it is wise to re-season before use.

TO SEASON UNENAMELLED IRON PANS

Scour the cold, dry utensil with a stiff brush and soapy water (*not detergent*), then rinse well and dry. Pour about a tablespoonful of salad oil or *unsalted* fat into the pan and spread it over all surfaces with a piece of cloth or paper towel. (Some prefer using a solid vegetable shortening, which must be unsalted, or lard, at this first stage.) Now add more oil, enough to cover the bottom of the pan, and set it over moderate heat until the oil is thin and hot, but not yet smoking. Remove the pan from the heat and tip it to swirl the oil about and cover bottom and sides. Add a little more oil and put the pan into an oven set to about 200–250°F, 110–130°C, gas mark ¼–½. Heat may be turned off after an hour but leave the pan in overnight. Remove, wipe off excess oil or rub it all over with a paper towel. It is now ready for use. Another method is to rub the cold, dry pan with lard or other unsalted solid fat, then heat very, very slowly. When quite hot, turn off heat but leave the pan in place. When cold, wipe off excess fat or rub it in well.

It should not, in normal handling, require re-seasoning until food burns on and sticks so the pan needs scouring; or if it should rust, it must be thoroughly cleaned and re-seasoned completely.

COOKING IN CAST IRON

This tedious care, and the added disadvantage of being so heavy to handle, make a cast-iron pot less desirable than one would wish. But, because it is thick, does not warp and will withstand intense heat – and retain it as well – it is excellent for browning and braising meats, for making good pot roasts and thick stews.

Acid foods (containing wine, tomatoes, pineapple, vinegar, fruit juices, etc.) such as *bœuf bourguignon* and *coq au vin* are best prepared in pans of other materials, such as enamelware and earthenware. I know that Grandma and her daughters made their stews in the old iron pot, but think again – did they add wine, or water or stock? If wine was added, it was towards the end of the cooking period, and the food was dished out as soon as it was ready, remember? Not only do acids tend to remove the seasoned layer, causing foods to stick and to darken unappetizingly, but they may cause a chemical reaction that results in unpleasant flavours and odours, as well. I don't chance it.

When the meal is quite done, the cook often takes a little

time to freshen up before dinner. She turns off the heat and feels quite safe in leaving. When she returns she finds that, if the food is in an iron pan with a domed lid, moisture has accumulated under the lid and dripped down into the food, causing it to separate and turn watery; and sometimes rust has formed on the inside of the lid. To avoid this catastrophe – and it can be that – simply remove the lid or cover only partially before going off to powder your nose.

It is not advisable to cook artichokes, potatoes or asparagus in iron pots, for iron discolours them.

The tendency to rust makes it vital to remove food from iron pots as soon as possible. This is also the reason why iron should never be left to soak.

It is generally believed that sprinkling a little salt into an iron or steel pan before cooking will prevent 'explosions' and keep the fat from sputtering and splattering over the stove. I use a little salt before grilling steaks and chops – it precludes the use of fat. Similarly, while making crêpes, if one should stick, remove as much as possible and rub in a very little salt and a few drops of oil. Wipe clean and the pan will be smooth and ready for the next crêpe.

CLEANING CAST IRON

My own method of cleaning cast iron is perhaps rather unorthodox, but it works for me. After braising, stewing or grilling, remove food immediately. With the heat off, but while the pan is still hot, pour in a little lukewarm water. No soap, certainly no detergent. Then, after the meal and before washing dishes, scrub the pan with a stiff brush, rinse it well and dry it immediately and thoroughly. If the oven is warm, leave it in the oven, or on a burner on the range for a few moments. A light coating of oil or a swish with some crumpled waxed paper, and I'm done.

Age and good care improve cast iron or sheet steel as the surface becomes saturated with oil and quite smooth, if properly cleaned. If you wrap a utensil for storage, do it loosely so air can get at it, and leave uncovered to avoid what is known as 'sweating', and consequent rust. Store in a dry place.

However, iron has a way of frustrating even the most zealous housekeeper. Rust can develop in spite of everything; even a spell of rainy weather can cause it. But, if rust develops or if food should burn and stick, all is not lost. Keep on hand some extra-fine steel-wool pads and a few sheets of 'fine' grade sandpaper, preferably the 'wet and dry' kind. Get a bar of old-fashioned yellow soap. Do not use liquid 'soaps' for I know none that is not detergent and *that* should never be used on iron for it removes the seasoning too thoroughly. (Keep the soap in an uncovered container; the secret of good soap is in exposure to air and ageing.) Have handy some *solid* unsalted fat: lard or suet from the butcher's.

Now, roll up your sleeves, don a good heavy apron, put some newspapers on the draining board and slip on your toughest rubber gloves. Rinse the iron utensil in hot water. Rub the steel wool over the bar of soap and get to work: rub, rub, rub all over until rust or burned-on food disappears and the surface feels perfectly smooth and even. Now, cut off a piece of sandpaper and rub some more. When the surface feels as smooth as your cheek, rinse thoroughly under running hot water and rinse again ... and again. Dry completely and put the pan over a burner on the range, at moderate heat. When nicely hot and free of all moisture, turn off heat and let pan cool just enough to handle. Then season with oil or fat as you would a new pan, preheat the oven to 250°F, 130°C, gas mark ½, turn off heat and set pan in the oven for several hours or overnight. It should be as good as new. Many otherwise intelligent and knowledgeable cooks advise the use of salt for cleaning iron and steel vessels, thus: 'Wipe clean with paper towelling and a little table salt ...' An astonishing bit of advice considering that even damp weather can rust a stored iron vessel and salt will become liquid with no help at all!

Steel

CARBON STEEL

Sheet-carbon steel, sometimes called 'high carbon steel', is the result of refining molten pig iron. It is used for a great variety of frying-pans, knife blades, bakeware and saucepans and it may be coated with tin, porcelain or enamel. Its value and price are influenced by its thickness and method of processing. Although it is less porous than cast

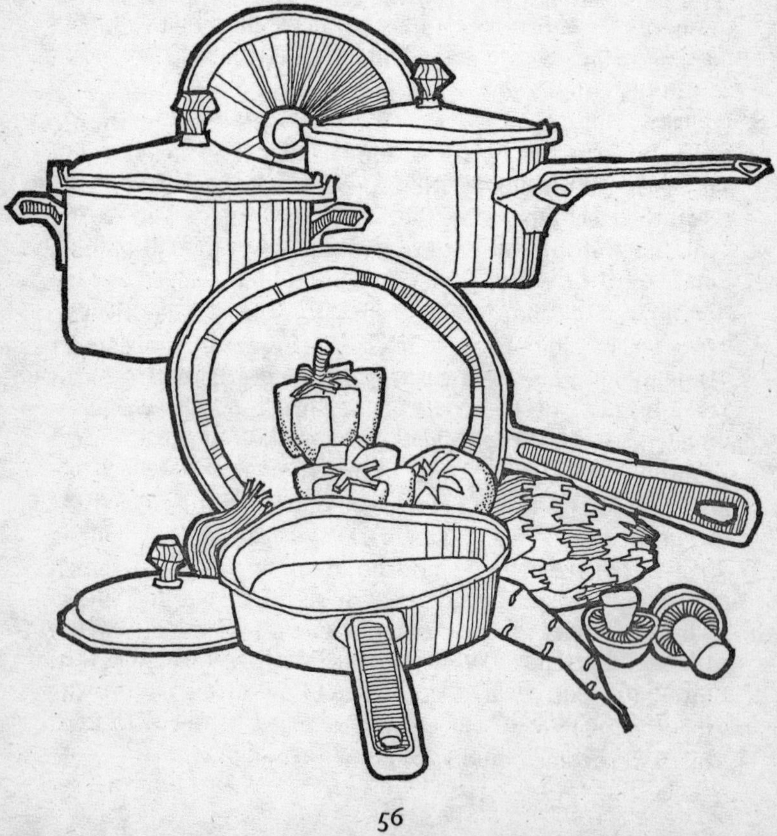

iron and more resistant to breakage, it does not conduct heat quite as evenly nor retain it as well. As it is so much thinner, it heats up very quickly, requiring greater care and attention. Like most sheet metal, it will warp when subjected to sudden changes of temperature. Do not pour cold water into a hot pan or take a steel pan from the refrigerator and set on high heat. Obviously, it is not nearly so desirable, nor will it always serve the same purpose, as the heavy cast-iron skillet.

CARE OF CARBON STEEL

A coating of lacquer is usually applied at the factory, to protect it from rusting. This coating must be removed before use. Set the carbon-steel pan in a large basin or pot, cover with water and bring to the boil. Simmer for ten minutes, then cool. When cool enough to handle, remove from the basin and scour it, inside and out, with a soapy steel-wool pad. Rinse thoroughly and dry well. Pour in a tablespoon of unsalted salad oil and heat it over moderate heat, just to the point where it is thin, but not yet smoking. Remove from heat and swirl the oil around to coat the entire surface, bottom and sides, then let it stand for some hours or overnight. Pour off excess oil and rub the pan dry. Wipe with paper towelling and store. Many pans now are 'pre-seasoned' at the factory and the manufacturers' directions will state this clearly, but do it anyway.

If the pan is used for only one purpose, such as cooking pancakes or omelettes or frying fish, then it usually requires only a brisk rubbing after each use. If it is washed with water, avoid using either soap or detergent and coat lightly with oil again. But if used for numerous purposes, it may well need thorough washing and re-seasoning afterwards.

A steel utensil should not be stored tightly covered at the risk of trapping moisture within and causing rust. If rust does develop, wash in hot soapy water and scour with fine steel wool, then re-season fully and carefully.

STEEL FRYING-PANS

A great variety of steel frying-pans is now available, many from France: omelette pans, crêpe pans, blini pans, and oval frying-pans, among them. They are made in various diameters: from 4 inches to 10–12 inches (or from 10 cm to 25–30 cm), depending on their intended use. These carbon-steel pans will last indefinitely if handled with care. Even professional French chefs prefer them to copper for everyday use, reserving copper for show-off work and for serving such elegant flambéed foods as crêpes Suzette, prepared over a burner before the diner.

French frying-pans have one particular great advantage over most others and that is in the matter of balance, a most vital consideration with these rather lightweight utensils with longish handles. Make the balance test: touch the handle end lightly, then let go ... of course, it will tip, but it *should* immediately right itself.

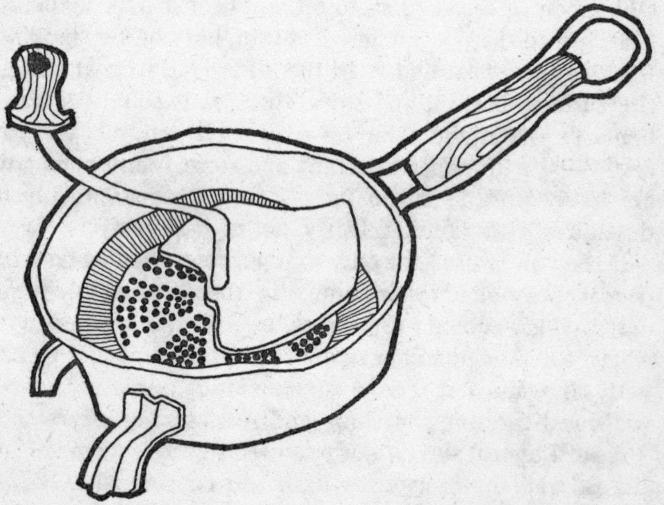

STAINLESS STEEL

Stainless steel is made by replacing some of the carbon in steel with chromium and nickel. Common stainless steel is designated as 18-8 to indicate that it is 18 parts chromium and 8 parts nickel. It must contain at least 11½ per cent chromium in order to be called 'stainless'.

Stainless steel has high-tensile strength, is not easily dented, is corrosion resistant, will take and hold a high polish, does not scratch with ordinary scouring and is not affected by food acids and alkalis. Its great disadvantage is that it does not conduct heat evenly, nor retain it well. This is why some firms cover the pan bottoms with copper or aluminium. Another way of improving heat conduction in a stainless-steel utensil is by putting a 'core' of another metal between two layers of stainless steel. Metals used in this way include iron, carbon steel and copper. However, unless these other-metal cores and bottom coatings are sufficiently thick, they cannot improve the basic weakness of stainless steel.

A thin steel pan, whether stainless or carbon steel, should never be preheated or it may warp. Start cooking over a medium flame and turn heat down as soon as the pan is satisfactorily heated. Never pour cold water into a hot pan or it will warp. Never use over high heat. Most modern pans do not require high heat for proper performance, and indeed care with heat can prolong the life of the pan almost indefinitely. Many stainless-steel pans have handles and knobs of plastic which can withstand heat up to 400°F, 200°C, but should never be subjected to higher heat or exposed to a direct flame as in grilling.

TERMS RELEVANT TO STAINLESS STEEL

Bottom clad: copper plated, or aluminium applied by spraying, to exterior bottoms.

Two-ply utensils have a coating of the other metal on either the entire interior or the entire exterior of the pan.

Three-ply utensils have the other metal between the interior and the exterior layers of the stainless steel somewhat like a copper, aluminium or steel 'sandwich'.

Stainless-steel ware is available in high-polish or 'satin' finish. Obviously the latter is more desirable in vessels to be used for cooking.

CARE OF STAINLESS STEEL

Stainless steel is used not only for cookware and bakeware, but for all kinds of implements and tools, among them knife blades. There are even stainless steel-wool pads which do not rust. Stainless steel in normal kitchen use is very easy to clean. Before using utensils for the first time, wash thoroughly with soap and water, to remove factory oils. Rinse well and dry. That's all.

If food has burned on and stuck, simply pour in enough water to cover the food and set pan over moderate heat; bring to the boil, turn off heat and allow it to stand until cool. It should be easy to remove then. Do not use abrasive cleaners, steel wool or a metal brush as they scratch the polished stainless-steel surface. If your stainless steel has acquired what is called 'heat tinting' from overheating, it can be removed with any good stainless-steel cleaner. Apply with a soft cloth and a light hand. Do not rub too hard or too briskly, as it is unnecessary and may scratch high polishes; rub in the direction of the polish lines. Follow directions on cleaners, rinse very thoroughly and wipe dry to avoid water marks.

Glass and Glass Ceramics

There are three main types of glass for kitchen use: *heat-proof* glassware for use at home-oven temperatures, such as pie plates, bread tins, roasting dishes, etc.; *flame-proof* glass vessels for surface cooking such as tea and water kettles, coffee pots, saucepans and skillets; and glass used for such equipment as mixing bowls, measuring cups, serving platters and refrigerator-storage dishes. These tolerate hot contents but not direct heat.

As these look much alike, it is vital that the cook know which type is being used and its limitations. Many are type-indicated on the glass (in raised or permanent lettering), but read the manufacturer's directions before buying to be certain you are getting the type you require.

Glass is one of the materials recommended for use in microwave ovens where even metal trimmings on glass may not be used.

COOKING IN GLASS

Since glass has low and uneven heat conductivity – but retains heat well – it is recommended for ovenware. Since foods bake faster in glass than in shiny metal, the temperature should be lowered by 25–35°F, or 10–20°C, from that suggested in the recipe, and until one is very experienced in its use, it should be watched very carefully. Lower heat generally is the best insurance for success with glass utensils.

Glass is non-porous and will not be affected by food acids or alkalis. It will not rust and is easily cleaned, though it can be scratched if scoured with abrasives or scrubbed carelessly with coarse metal pads. A very fine steel-wool pad may be used lightly, if necessary. Once scratched, cleaning becomes more difficult and food sticks more readily.

Many feel that acid foods such as fruits, fruit sauces and tomatoes have better and purer flavour if prepared in a glass saucepan. Coffee, too, is said to taste better if made in a glass (or enamel) pot; many will never use metal for it nor for tea. To repeat, no material is ideal for all purposes, and that applies here, as well. Covers on glass utensils do not fit snugly and more liquid must be used to avert the danger of burning and subsequent shattering.

Flame-proof glass should be protected with an iron grid set between heating unit and pan. Using the iron grid will also improve the heat-conducting properties. It should be remembered that, although flame-proof glass will take rather high temperatures, it will not withstand sudden sharp changes in temperatures nor is it shatterproof; it will break if dropped. Glass utensils that are flame-proof may, of course, also be used for ovenware. But heat-resistant glass – meant only for oven use – may not be used for surface cooking on a flame or an electric unit; many say that an asbestos pad or heat distributor will protect heat-proof glass, but it is not advisable to use it even in this way.

TYPES OF GLASSWARE

'Pyrex' is not a generic name for heat-resistant glass; it is a patented trade name for Corning Glass Company's product. Corningware, their opaque glass-ceramic pans that are flame- and heat-resistant, may safely be moved from stove to refrigerator and vice versa and then used for serving. Their usual detachable handle converts all pans to casseroles, happily. On a much smaller scale, other companies are now producing similar products.

There is now a small frying-pan in the Corningware range. It resembles the classic omelette pan and has – most unusual for Corning products – a permanent handle. This pan, when used on low heat, is excellent for cooking omelettes, blinis, pancakes, all kinds of fried eggs. Food should be removed from the pan as soon as it is cooked to the desired state, for the pan retains heat so well that the food continues to cook.

Ceramic-top cookers and ceramic hobs are now becoming more and more popular. These have a glass top with the cooking elements underneath. They do require that a perfectly flat-bottomed pan be used, and glass ceramic products are the perfect utensils for use on them. The hobs or cookers require little more cleaning than a wipe over the top! And as the heating coils are set close together, the problem of poor heat conductivity in glass is minimized. They may be used as work-tops when cold.

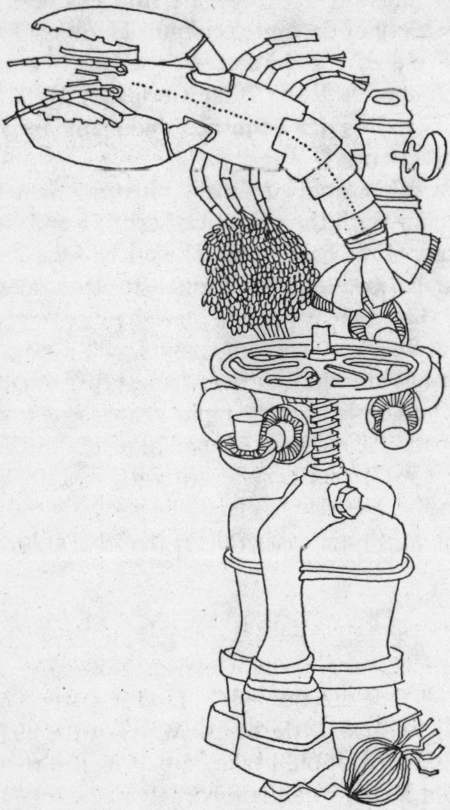

Vitreous Enamel

Vitreous enamel or enamel are interchangeable terms for a glasslike substance fused to steel, iron or aluminium. It may crack or chip if handled carelessly, but, when used with care, will last a long time and give highly satisfactory service. If the base metal is thin, the coating will chip more readily. A fine crack is easily widened and, unless the base is aluminium, rust will develop and spread.

There are many grades and qualities of vitreous enamel; seeing a large selection will point up the finer grades promptly. Almost every cookware firm has now a line of them in a variety of decorator colours. Many very attractive and heavy pieces are imported from such countries as France, Belgium, Ireland, West Germany, Holland and a number of Scandinavian countries, and many are, of course, made in this country.

Like any other applied finish, vitreous-enamel utensils vary in quality with the amount of coating and the quality and thickness of the base metal. The price of the utensil may or may not indicate quality, though it often does; we can be certain that a heavy-gauge steel base, covered with a few coats of fine, very smooth enamel, will not be cheap.

Research has greatly improved these types of coating and increased their resistance to rapid changes of temperature and to impact. Many new enamel-like substances such as polyamide plastic and acrylic are very practical; they do not chip easily, are easy to clean and can be fused to lighter gauges of aluminium, making them available at lower prices.

USING ENAMELWARE

Enamelware is very easily cleaned. Normally, soap and water are all that are needed. If food has stuck or burned on, soaking with a little soapy water, to which a little ammonia is added, should take care of it. If a roaster, used in high oven heats, has a stubborn stain or foods stuck to it, I sometimes spray on a little 'window cleaner' (the kind with ammonia added) and leave it on for a while. It seems to do the trick. Plastic scouring pads, used with soap or detergent, are also helpful. Do not use metal scouring pads for they tend to scratch the smooth finish; it will be more difficult to clean later and foods will stick more readily.

As noted earlier, many cooks will not use a metal pan for making a white sauce or a sauce requiring the addition of fruit juices or wine, and consider an enamel-coated pan the perfect utensil. It will not change the colour of foods nor the flavour. The main danger lies – as it does with china and glass – in cracking, breaking or chipping on impact with a very hard object; striking with a metal implement or dropping on a stone or tile floor. To stay on the safe side, only wooden or plastic spoons and stirrers should be used in enamel-coated pans.

A very interesting innovation has been brought to my attention. I am told, on excellent authority, that the entire Le Creuset line from France is now made with two special layers of enamel: the first is matte black with which the iron base is so thoroughly impregnated that should the second, outer layer (of coloured enamel) chip, the iron base is still protected and will not rust. Also, the manufacturer assures the importer that all imperfect pans are destroyed.

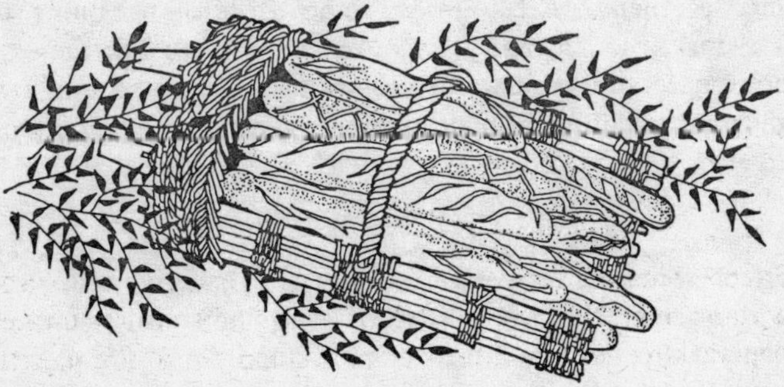

Clay

Ceramics, terracotta, heat-proof china and porcelain are all clay products and there is a long list of trade names to designate the various kinds. They vary enormously but the chief differences lie in the quality of the clay, the methods of processing and the glazes used in finishing.

They are opaque products, more or less coarse in texture (the earthenware more than the china) resulting in a porous product. Most are not affected by foods but are by sudden changes in temperature.

Earthenware has served many purposes throughout the years. The very first cooking utensil was made of clay and many refinements have been developed over the centuries. Many terracotta utensils that have come back into fashion are influenced by very early ones, such as those found in ancient Etruscan tombs; they look much like split wig stands. Others are shaped like chickens or fish, some are covered with hieroglyphic symbols. All these are more or less porous and often unglazed, though they may have a glaze inside or outside, rarely both, and are generally referred to as 'bricks'.

USE AND CARE OF EARTHENWARE

Since earthenware is porous, some form of seasoning is necessary, though many pans are now pre-seasoned at the factory. The method I was taught a long time ago was to wash off all dust, then dry well; rub all over with a cut clove of garlic and fill the pot with water. Add a few bay leaves, a few peppercorns, some pickling spices and whatever other herbs and spices you prefer. Set the pot over an asbestos pad on very low heat and bring *slowly* to a mere simmer. Simmer *gently* for about half an hour, then turn off the heat but let the pan stand until completely cool. Pour off liquid and dry well.

A pot seasoned in this way may then be used for surface cooking, but always on an asbestos pad or heat distributor. Turn heat on only after setting the pot on the burner. A ceramic pot does not require high heat, ever. When removing pots from heat (surface or oven) set on a dry surface. Be certain pots are room temperature before putting into a stove or oven. A cold pot is almost sure to crack if subjected to sharp changes in temperature.

Many of us are deeply attracted to primitive and home-crafted ceramics. However, a number of cases of lead poisoning have been traced to primitive Mexican pottery and to pottery made by amateurs in classes. This is caused by improper handling of the common lead glaze, and is a very serious danger indeed. There is no way short of using very highly technical machinery to discover which is hazardous and which is not. Therefore, if a question exists, do not use the receptacle for foods, especially those containing acids such as fruit juices and wine or coffee. These pieces should be used for decorative purposes only, or to hold nuts (with shells), or as ashtrays.

PORCELAIN

Another type of clayware is ovenproof porcelain or china. It is made by several companies throughout the world, and is used for soufflé dishes, *gratin* dishes, *pots à crème*, quiche dishes, ramekins, etc. This ware is cleaned much like any fine china and it takes little knowledge to know that it should be at room temperature before going into an oven, that the heat should be moderate or low and that the dish should be removed with care and set down on a dry, warm surface. Do not use directly over a flame or an electric burner unless specifically labelled as 'flame-proof'.

CERAMICS

There are also the rather 'soft' glazed ceramic ovenproof vessels. They require tender handling though not so much as to be a nuisance. I have known some to be in use in Europe for well over twenty-five years. They are used for baking and grilling, and are very convenient and inexpensive.

Stoneware is a ceramic that has been 'fired' to very high temperature for a long time, so that it has greater density and approaches the hardness of glass or stone. Many domestic and imported casseroles are of this ware. When thumped with the middle finger flicked from the thumb (as one does to test crystal) it has a clear and sharp sound; softer earthenware sounds duller. Often this type is glazed on the inside but left unglazed on the outside. It is generally higher priced than softer clayware, is not affected by foods and will not absorb odours or flavours as some softer wares do. The best of this ware is from Vallauris in southern France, though many interesting and fine pieces are now being produced in this country.

Non-Stick Coatings

When the new non-stick coatings first appeared on the market, I was, like all of us who think in terms of diets and weight problems, all fired up about this amazing material on which one could cook without added fats. I immediately bought a fine, heavy-gauge aluminium frying-pan coated with the lovely bisque-coloured material as lining. I also bought some nylon implements to use on it, as the directions suggested.

The first morning I cooked bacon and scrambled eggs and was happy as a lark. Nothing stuck; I just rinsed it afterwards. Of course, pancakes looked sort of lean, dry and uneven. But I didn't mind. Steaks were rather grey for they had to be cooked over moderate heat. When food began to stick not too long after I had bought it, I bought some 'paint' to touch up the scratches, but there weren't any; I really had been careful. It was very disappointing. I returned to the old butter routine, gained a little weight and finally went back to my old cast iron.

I cannot remember that a suggestion was made to 'season' the lining; of course I should have known better. It is a porous material, so requires treating.

When the 'durable' linings appeared, off I went to get a new pan. No, I did not use ordinary metal implements as the manufacturer assured me I could; I used wooden ones (I like them better, anyway). But I did notice that the label suggested giving the lining a coat of oil and I have done that ever since. I have now been using the 'durable' for five and a half months and a heavier coating of oil seems necessary as time passes. The coating is rather scratched and the little 'pebbles' that stick up seem to have become flatter. But it's a lovely form and I'm getting used to it. As long as I coat it with grease it works like a charm.

If I sound disenchanted, it may be because I am. Non-stick coatings, I have learned, just don't last as long as the metal pans they are put on. So buy a good heavy pan you'll enjoy using later without the coating.

Non-stick pans are coated with fluoro-carbon resin, which is sprayed on and heat-treated. The natural material is white, but colours are added to minimize the inconvenience of staining.

Some utensil manufacturers assure the consumer that, with proper care, experimental pans coated with non-stick linings have been used for eight to ten years and are still easy to clean and give good service. But one of the biggest manufacturers of non-stick utensils includes in its literature the statement: 'Because of possible abuses, no manufacturer can guarantee the life of the coating.'

The new 'durables' are supposed to be much more scratch-resistant than the ordinary non-stick linings. I have spoken to many housewives about the durables and have used quite a few in friends' homes. We all feel that they have sacrificed a little of the slickness for a longer-lasting coating. They definitely require a coating of oil after and before every use. Though the small pebbles that stand up and take the brunt of punishment do save the lower areas, there seems little gained. One is warned not to use 'hard-edged metal tools' on the lining, but I think it is safest to avoid metal altogether and to continue to use wooden and nylon implements.

Government tests have found non-stick linings perfectly safe, for any chemicals that are absorbed by food are ingested in such small quantities that they represent no danger. Tests have shown that most of the chemicals that will be removed from the lining during cooking are removed the first time a pan is used. So if you want to be extra careful, it is a good idea to boil some water and washing-up liquid in a new pan for a few minutes. Then rinse very thoroughly and use as normal.

USE AND CARE OF NON-STICK LININGS

For cleaning non-stick linings, soap and hot water should be sufficient, but nylon or polyester-based scrubbers are available. Be sure to recondition the pan with a light coating of oil.

Should the non-stick lining become discoloured, darkened or stained, it can be cleaned with a mild bleach solution. The Dupont Company which produces the Teflon linings gives instructions for cleaning in its care-and-use leaflet. Discoloration is caused by grease and food stains that have settled into the pores, carbonizing and discolouring the coating and it can affect the non-stick qualities of the lining. The manufacturers assure us that 'after proper cleaning and re-oiling, the lining regains its non-stick properties'. Some lines do offer re-coating within a certain time limit, at 'reasonable' expense. I am told the expense of relining comes very close to the cost of a new pan.

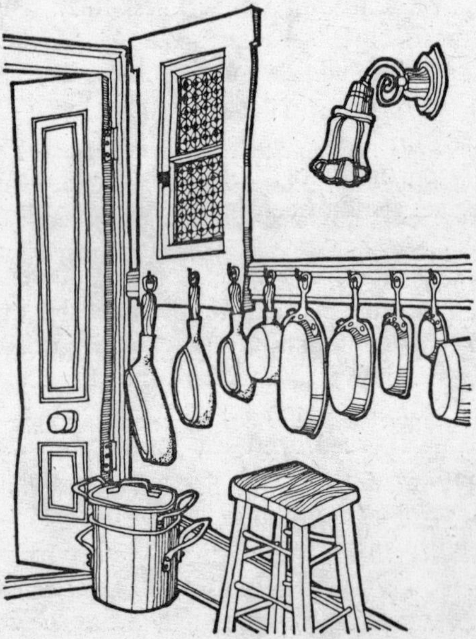

Aluminium

Thousands of years ago, prehistoric man made his first successful cooking utensil of a clay made up largely of hydrated silicate of aluminium. But the widespread use of aluminium for kitchenware did not start until very recently. In the nineteenth century a number of European and American scientists began trying to separate aluminium from the compound in which it occurs. In the 1850s, the French started production in limited quantities; one of its earliest applications was a set of spoons and forks for Napoleon III, who cherished them more than his gold and silver.

The big breakthrough towards mass production came in 1886. Charles Martin Hall, a twenty-two-year-old American, working in the shed behind his father's house, succeeded in separating aluminium, using the electrolytic process. Simultaneously, a Frenchman, Paul L. T. Héroult, working independently in France, made the same discovery.

TYPES OF ALUMINIUM

Cooking utensils are made from either cast or sheet aluminium, usually with another metal added, such as magnesium or copper, for hardness. Casting aluminium results in durable, heavy utensils, completely without seams. It is particularly desirable for 'waterless' and surface cookery and is used for skillets, griddles, casseroles and pressure cookers. It is, however, more porous than sheet metal and has a tendency to pit more readily. Cast utensils are distinguishable from sheet-metal utensils by two features: (1) The rim has a straight edge, rounded and smoothed. (2) The handle, or shank for the handle, is cast in one piece with the body of the pan.

Sheet or drawn aluminium is made by rolling heavy-gauge sheets under intense pressure, then stretching them into the desired shape. The rolling increases the density and durability of the metal and its uniform thickness. A heavily rolled sheet is harder and more resistant to pitting, warping and denting. The finer the grain produced, the finer the product. Saucepans and kettles are made of varying gauges of sheet aluminium. Baking tins, moulds, measuring cups and other implements are also made from sheet aluminium, usually much thinner. Sheet aluminium can be dented, but it is not easily broken; cast aluminium can be broken upon severe impact.

A commercial aluminium available in restaurant-supply stores is impregnated with silicone, which results in a lovely gunmetal colour. The silicone prevents pitting and oxidizing (darkening) resulting from chemicals in food and water, it is flavourless and does not affect food in any way. However, the process is expensive and the pans are dear.

CARE AND USE OF ALUMINIUM

Aluminium is very effective for cooking purposes because of its ability to conduct heat quickly and evenly. Experts repeatedly insist that good aluminium pots be heavy and thick. Because aluminium is such a good conductor of heat, the heat will transfer too rapidly in thin pans, causing the food to stick and burn. To avoid this, all cooking (except the simple boiling of water) in thinner pans should be started at low heat. Thin pans will also dent and warp more readily, causing uneven cooking.

Although aluminium does not rust, it is pitted by alkalis and a few acids, causing tiny holes in the surface of the metal. Alkalis also tarnish or darken the metal, but this discoloration is removed when acid foods such as apples, rhubarb or tomatoes are cooked in the pan. A pan can also be brightened by simmering in it for ten to fifteen minutes a solution of vinegar and water or two teaspoonfuls of cream of tartar to each quart (or litre) of water. This tarnish or darkening is not in any way harmful and does not change the properties of foods cooked in the pan, nor does it affect the acid foods cooked to remove the tarnish. They may be eaten safely. A good scrubbing with a soapy steel-wool pad is also effective to shine your pans, but be sure to rinse very thoroughly with hot water and to dry promptly and well. Since dull or dark materials absorb heat rather than reflect it, count your blessings if your pans are not quite as shiny as new.

When cleaning aluminium, let pans cool before filling with soapy water; cool water may well warp hot pans. A warped pan can be corrected to some degree in the following way: heat the empty pan for about ten minutes, then turn it upside down on a flat surface and set a block of wood on the upturned bottom; strike the wood with a hammer until the bottom is again level.

IS ALUMINIUM SAFE?

Some people like copper, some don't. Some like iron, others won't use it. Some love stainless steel and will use nothing else; others couldn't care less. But *aluminium* causes passions to flare: it's loathed or it's loved.

In my quest for some resolution to the aluminium controversy, I visited twelve health-food shops and read an infinite number and variety of books and articles. I've corresponded with scientific and research laboratories and agencies of every description: for nutrition, metallurgy, agriculture, ecology. Fourteen different nutritionists and home economists working in widely distant places in the United States promptly replied that they would recommend aluminium, for it was in essence a 'friendly' element and harmless to the body. All were connected with highly respected organizations involved in preparation and experimentation with food and food containers.

One food writer advises that aluminium should not be used to cook eggs when the eggs are in direct contact with the metal. Other authorities, however, *do* recommend aluminium for omelettes. For example, there is the James Beard omelette pan.

While there are those who feel that aluminium is not a safe metal to cook with, government researchers regard it as safe, and a communication from the American Food and Drug Administration says: '... There is an abundance of evidence that cooking in aluminum utensils is harmless ... Aluminum is the third most abundant element in the earth's crust ... [and] occurs naturally in many foods. Also, aluminum compounds have a number of uses as direct food ingredients, as for example, in alum baking powders ... These uses are generally recognized as safe by scientists qualified to evaluate the safety of food additives.' The report concludes that 'many scientific studies have determined that the amount of aluminum ingested as a result of preparing foods in aluminum cookware, even when soda is used in the cooking, is so small as to be of no significance in comparison with the amount of aluminum consumed from other sources.'

In all my search for information, I can't say I'm truly convinced there's anything wrong with aluminium, except for one factor, and not one word have I found about that: the accumulation of matter in pitted aluminium. I've seen pans being used that were so pitted one's fingers could feel the ridges. If one cleaned such a pan casually and did not get rid of accumulated food in the pits, it could become a breeding ground for bacteria. My suggestions then are that, if an aluminium pan is badly pitted, dented and warped, you relegate it to gardening use or just throw it out. If you must use it, wash it in an electric dishwasher or scrub with a long-bristled stiff brush with a little disinfectant added, and rinse thoroughly.

Batterie de Cuisine

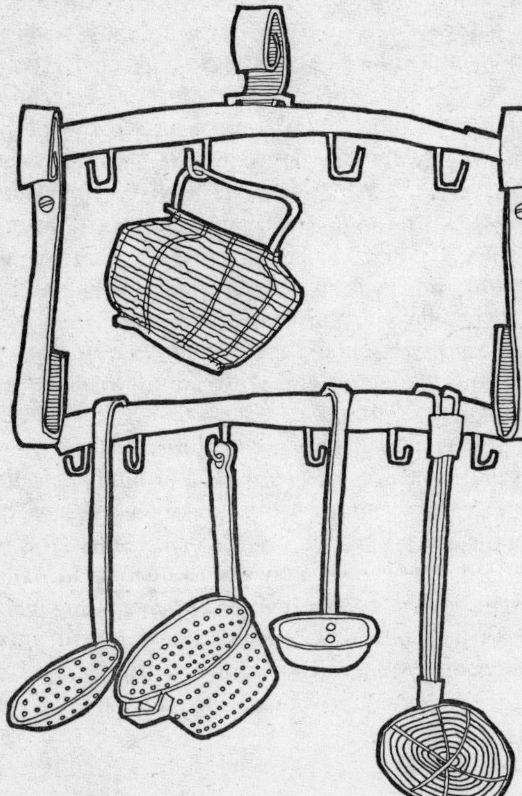

This chapter will deal with selecting the *batterie de cuisine*, which includes every kind of cooking aid from saucepans to beaters, from jelly moulds to kettles, from knives to graters and so on. This is the alternative to Cleopatra's twelve kitchens: a crew of kitchen helpers to keep food in good condition while even the most long-winded poet has the floor.

There is no doubt that a large part of the convenience and pleasure of working in a kitchen depends on the equipment in it. The choice of pots and pans, etc., may directly affect the results obtained. The flavour, visual appeal and even the nutritive value of food may be improved by them. Although it is perfectly possible to create a fine meal in an inconvenient, ill-equipped and drab kitchen, it is far easier to do so in a colourful, convenient and well-equipped kitchen.

Selecting the equipment for your kitchen is much like choosing a lover or a mate; it is necessary to weigh the advantages against the disadvantages, and vice versa. The experts can tell you what is efficient and what inefficient and why. But no one can possibly know what *you* like, how many people *you* must cook for, what kind of heat source *you* have, the size of *your* kitchen and storage space, nor even how much weight *you* can lift or how much money *you* can spend!

As to design, if Bauhaus or Pop turns you on, you will probably find all-white kitchenware absolutely irresistible. If herb gardens are *you*, then it's copperware and cast iron, and hang the trouble! If you never make omelettes, you'll not need an omelette pan, no matter how chic your friends think them. And, if you breakfast in a floating peignoir trimmed with maribou, you're not likely to enjoy frying eggs in a cast-iron spider. It's as simple as that.

Some time ago the *New York Times* carried an article by Craig Claiborne, concerning the reopening of one of the best-stocked cookware shops in the U.S.A.: Fred Bridges in New York City. Mr Claiborne related that a local socialite telephoned the shop in great distress, for she was serving beef stroganoff for forty guests and 'my chef needs something suitable to cook it in'. Mr Bridges advised her to get a brazier 'a wide one or it comes out mush. I've got just what you want and it costs $105.00, but I'll let you have it for $95.00.' Madame was furious: 'Are you out of your mind? Do you think I'm made of money?' To which Mr Bridges calmly replied that he did not, but she should buy 'the best, and you wouldn't give a thought to buying a dress for $200 ...' 'But I could wear the dress,' she retorted. 'You could wear the brazier if you strapped it on your back,' he promptly returned. Mr Claiborne goes on to say that she bought the brazier and took great pleasure in telling the story to her guests.

My point in retelling the story is to reassert that most cooking vessels cost no more than many other articles bought every day without a second thought for the price, and often less. No woman I know would wear the same dress three times a week for ten years; a good sturdy cooking vessel can be used seven days a week, twice a day, for an entire lifetime, and then be an heirloom for another generation.

In general, the *batterie de cuisine* is grouped into three large classifications: utensils for surface cookery, utensils for oven cookery and tools or implements used in preparing foods. In selecting utensils for your home, it is wise to remember that a single utensil that will serve a number of purposes is preferable to utensils that will do only one job each. For example, a saucepan with a removable handle will also double as a casserole. But do not carry this so far that you leave yourself without the necessary pans when preparing an elaborate meal.

Each implement should be judged on efficiency and durability of material and construction as well as the care it will require. The material, size and shape should suit the purpose for which the implement is being chosen. It should be simple in design to facilitate cleaning and easy to operate so that it will accomplish the job to be done without great effort and in a reasonable amount of time.

'A little pot/Is soon hot' was popular advice during the last century and may well be revived now. It refers to the silly habit of using a large pot when a small one will serve the purpose, save on fuel and cost less all round.

Unless you can promise yourself that, no matter how dire the circumstances, you will never, never, never use a metal tool or wire whisk or an eggbeater on the following types of cookware, don't use them at all! It's sacrilege. (1) *Silver or tin-lined copperware,* thick or thin. (2) *Porcelain or enamel,* no matter what the base metal or how strong the manufacturer says they are, or how casually he assures you they may be treated. (3) *Resin-lined, non-stick pans,* even those guaranteed to be scratch-proof, scuff-proof and stain-resistant. These are all expensive and delicate instruments.

If it is your habit, when in a fury, to hurl pots and pans, use cheap, thin ones (they bounce better and make a more satisfactory sound) and forget serious cooking.

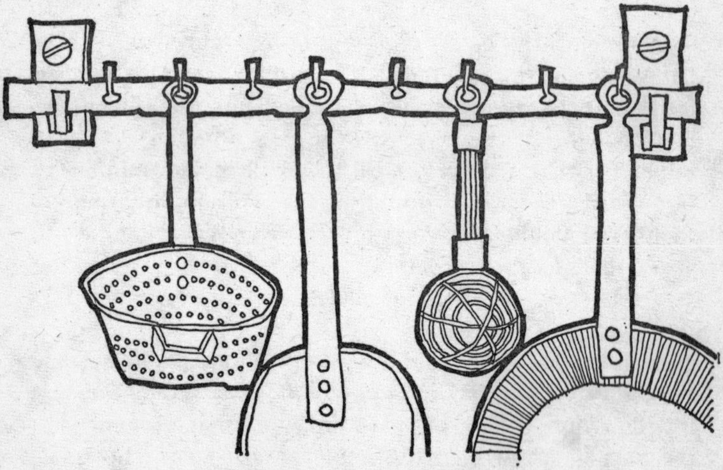

LIDS

A lid should fit securely but still afford space for steam to escape. It should be as heavy as the pan itself. It should have a lip or flange of some kind to prevent condensed steam or escaping moisture from dripping down the outside of the pan. Any heavy pan with a well-fitting lid may be used for 'waterless cooking'; the lid should seal in all moisture so food cooks in its own juices and bastes itself. Knobs on lids should be securely attached but, if made of a material that can erode, easy to replace. They should be of heat-resistant material and shaped for convenience, not just for looks. Knobs should be easy to grasp and hold, even with oily or wet fingers. Some of the newer designs are very exciting to look at, but under pressure of use are not at all practical. It is essential that pans be lifted and handled *before purchase* (one of the main arguments against mail-order buying).

Some lids are fitted with handles instead of knobs and can be used as shallow pans. The handles should be designed so that they will not burn and be of heat-resistant material.

Most good heavy utensils have practical lids. It is with the lighter ware that one must really be careful. As mentioned earlier, glassware has ill-fitting lids, but the handles are usually detachable and very practical for oven use. One of the disadvantages of otherwise desirable earthenware is that pieces often come without covers or with lids that are warped and ill-fitting. Both primitive and modern pieces often have impractical lid knobs that simply slip through the fingers. Most cast ironware and cast aluminium ware have well-fitting lids, though the handles are usually out of balance, too short and of non-heat-resisting material, alas.

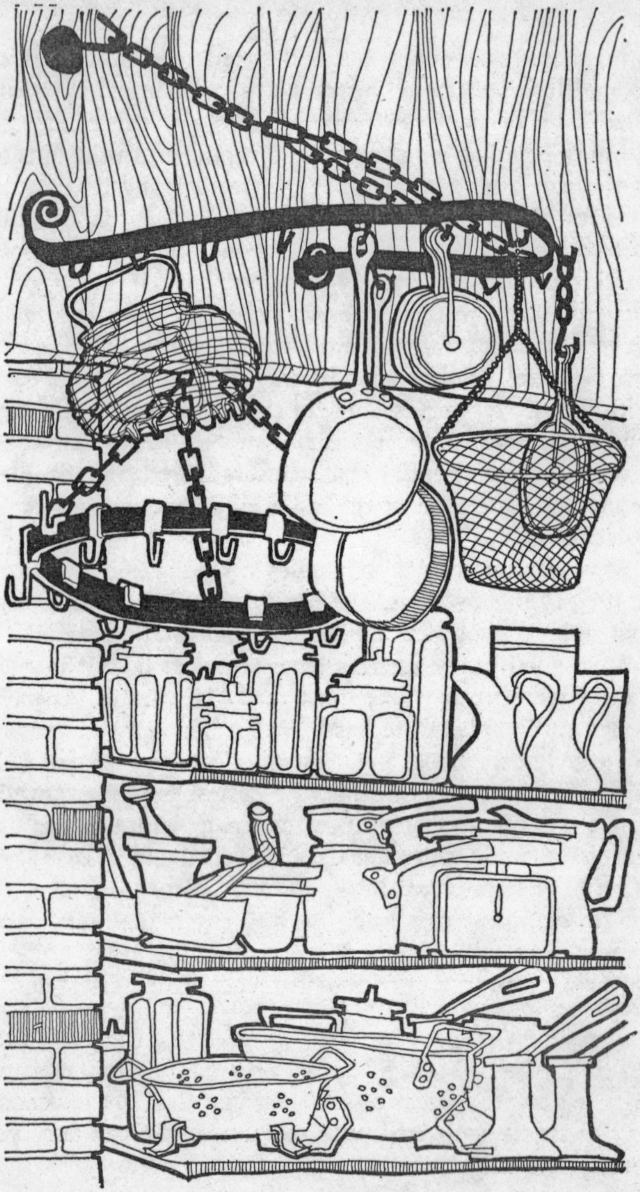

HANDLES

The handle of a pan is not, by any means, the least important part of the utensil. A carelessly made handle, carelessly attached, will indicate a carelessly made pot, at any price. It should not be too heavy for the pan or it will force the pan to tip over easily; if it is too light it may give or bend when a full pan is lifted. The *balance test* will give some indication of this: remove the lid and tap the end of the handle. The pan should tip backwards but right itself immediately. Grip the pan by the handle, turn it upside down and shake to be sure the handle is secure. Check that *removable* handles are easy to remove and replace, and that they grip the pan securely.

Wood is a good material for handles since it is heat-resistant, impervious to moisture (unless constantly soaked) and resistant to slipping. Teak is probably the most fire-resistant of all woods. Many woods are today impregnated with a heat-resistant substance. Be sure that the underside of the handle is covered with metal near the pan and protected from the burner.

Wooden knobs and handles should never be left to soak. They should be removed before washing and hand-cleaned. Detergents should not be used on them (they tend to dry out the wood), and they should never be washed in an automatic dishwasher.

Since handles are made in many shapes and forms, they should fit the hand of the user and be comfortable. Never forget that the handle of a pan is the part you touch most often; you can learn to loathe a pan if its handle is painful to touch.

One of the best methods for attaching metal handles is by electric welding, which permanently fuses the metal parts. (It can be identified by tiny, barely visible spots on the inside of the pan and on the exterior where the handle joins the base.) When rivets are used to attach handles, they are generally secure, but are easier to clean on coated ware, when they are covered. On old-fashioned pots and some primitive pans, rivets are handmade and very uneven. Soldered handles are not very strong and the vessel should not be expected to take great strain or intense heat.

Handles on less expensive pans present various problems. Be sure there are no rough edges to tear at your hand. Be sure the seam, if 'turned', is smooth, so dirt, food and grease cannot collect in the crevices. If it is a single bar of metal, be sure the edges are dull and rounded.

Frequent inspection of handles and knobs should become a habit with homemakers. A loosened handle, spotted during cleaning, can avert a disaster. Special attention should be given to points of connection and attachment under the handle joint; they become quite unsanitary if food, grease and dirt are permitted to collect in the crevices. An old toothbrush is a very handy instrument for reaching these otherwise inaccessible spots.

SPOUTS

Spouts are usually welded to the body of the utensil so smoothly that most people are not even aware they were once quite separate pieces, and that's as it should be. Spouts should be carefully inspected at the time of purchase. They should be shaped in such a way that the liquid runs down the centre dip (or rounded fold) and cannot spill over the sides. The edge or rim should be thin and it should be sharp enough to prevent dripping or dribbling down the side of the pot. The spout should be cleaned – and often – with a brush small enough to fit into the curve.

Utensils for Surface Cookery

In addition to the cardinal points outlined in the chapter on materials, the features to watch for in a kitchen utensil are, unfortunately, many. For most ordinary uses, a pan should have a flat, level bottom that meets the vertical sides in a gentle curve. A sharp angle is more difficult to clean and a nuisance when stirring thick mixtures of food like puddings and sauces. The top rim should be smooth and not so sharp or thin as to be a hazard. If the rim is 'beaded' or rolled over (in a sheet-metal pan) it should be as flat as possible. In thin metal pans this 'beading' tends to lend sturdiness to the pan and helps it to take wear and tear. But a crevice here collects grease and dirt.

The pan should be well balanced. This is most important: imbalance has been the cause of many serious kitchen accidents. Before purchasing, do the balance test described in the previous section on handles. There is also the matter of it being the right weight for *you*; pick it up in the shop, with the cover and without. Put your purse into it or a small bowl and see how that *feels*. Be sure it is not uncomfortably heavy. *Left-handed cooks* should look for pans and skillets with *two* pouring lips. They do exist, so demand them.

SAUCEPANS, FRYING-PANS, CASSEROLES AND KETTLES

All of the vessels used for surface cookery today, and available in so many materials, shapes and sizes, are the descendants of the cauldron, one of the most important household utensils since the Bronze Age. Made of bronze and later of cast iron, the cauldron was originally suspended over the fire by two ring handles. Gradually it became more squat in shape, developed three tapering legs and either a long handle or a movable hoop handle (bail) from which it hung over the fire, and a flat lid with a raised rim.

The cauldron was set into the hearth or among coals in the fire (when not hanging over it) and more coals were heaped on the rimmed lid. It served a multitude of purposes: for baking bread, biscuits and cake, for cooking stews and boiling soups, for fricasseeing small game and chickens, for simmering beans and making conserves. It was a most valued possession; many families had no other cooking vessel.

Water vessels with spouts, which were suspended over the fire by a bail, were a relatively early variation on the cauldron. A fifteenth-century example is to be found in the British Museum. Our stove kettle is very similar to these early models.

With the advent of the modern kitchen range in the early nineteenth century, the cauldron lost its legs and developed into our casserole, used for surface as well as oven cooking. (The American name for the large iron pot which we generally term a casserole is 'Dutch oven', which can be confusing as the English Dutch oven was a curved metal screen which was placed in front of the fire and in which meat was hung.)

Our saucepan and frying-pan both developed from the skillet, the cauldron with a long handle. Today's skillets or frying-pans are, in essence, shallow saucepans. They should be made of materials that conduct heat rapidly and evenly and in a gauge heavy enough to prevent denting and warping. Have you ever tried to make pancakes on a warped skillet? It's not really funny. A test should be made in the shop before buying: place a pencil across the bottom of the pan and if there is even the tiniest space under the pencil, reject it! Cast iron or aluminium, fireproof or flameproof glass are the most desirable materials since they are most warp resistant.

A variation on the skillet is the chicken-fryer or *sautoir* which is shaped much like a very deep frying-pan, usually having sides about 4 inches (10 cm) high. I find this shape has infinite possibilities as a stew-pan or a casserole. It should have a domed lid for extra capacity and a handle or shank cast with the pan (if it is of a cast material). My favourite material in this form is copper, particularly for fricassees and stews. These forms for surface cookery are dealt with in the section 'Exotica (page 112).

DOUBLE BOILERS

The double boiler is essential for many tasks in which very slow cooking is necessary of delicate foods that need emulsifying: puddings and sauces primarily. For mixtures that contain vinegar, fruits and wine, the best materials are glass, flame-proof ceramics and vitreous enamels. I have seen one lovely one that combines copper and thick porcelain; however, it is not only outrageously expensive, but impractical for making sauces since it heats up too rapidly, having little space between the upper pan and copper bottom. It is usually assumed that double boilers can be used as two separate saucepans; this porcelain top is not flameproof! In short, if you are attracted to it as the moth to the flame, by all means buy it, but put it on your highest shelf and leave it there – for ever!

A good double boiler is two saucepans, slightly different in size and shape. However, the practice of using any small pan with any large pan is not only hazardous but foolish. If one must do this, there are adjustable racks with handles that at least hold the smaller pan securely in place. After taking great pains with a sauce, involving, perhaps, expensive ingredients, all can be lost by a careless movement of the hand, resulting in a lost sauce, lost time and possibly a burned hand.

No such object as a double boiler exists in France. They wisely set a bowl into a very slightly larger saucepan filled with water, for the same purpose, and call it a *bain-marie.*

PRESSURE COOKERS

The pressure cooker developed from the bulky old home canner that was such a boon to the farmer's wife. It has become an accepted part of the *batterie de cuisine* and is now available in many different materials and combinations of materials. In general meal preparation, it shortens many cooking processes and cooks food with amazing rapidity. However, overcooking for even a few moments can result in a mushy mess, so close attention is required.

Among the reasons for using a pressure cooker is the retention of water-soluble vitamins owing to the absence of air during cooking, the small amount of liquid added and the brief cooking period. Natural colour and flavour are also better retained and shrinkage is minimized. In the cooking of less expensive and tougher cuts of meat, pressure cooking tends to soften tough tissues. A final reason is economy of fuel consumption.

True, pressure cookers are expensive. They also require very careful cleaning. But the pressure pan can be used without the pressurizing mechanism and proves an excellent saucepan with its well-fitting cover and steam-escape hole.

Cooking time is counted from the moment the desired pressure is reached; at the end of the prescribed time, pressure is returned to normal before lifting the lid. The usual method is to run cold water over the pan, unless the model has a special device for releasing steam. It is preferable, with such foods as meat and dried vegetables, to let the pressure return slowly. It has been suggested that with foods that thicken liquids (cereals, beans, stew, etc.) the pan be placed in cold water to cool the bottom of the cooker as well. Obviously, careful study of directions for care is essential.

Baking

The steadily increasing interest in home bread-baking is a very exciting phenomenon, whether one uses a lovely old wooden bread trough, primitive ceramics, glistening glass, porcelain or stainless steel; an electric oven or a classic brick oven (as I did once upon a legendary time in a fantasy house named Crazy Crescent).

Baking bread, with time and practice, becomes a completely creative act. One starts with a standard recipe of a traditional bread and soon learns to set a part of the dough aside for improvising variations: adding herbs or spices or more fat and sugar, cinnamon or raisins; or one learns to experiment and bake on a new long roofing tile or in new tiny flower pots or coffee cans. One plays with shapes: braiding, rolling, slashing in patterns, and soon the bread one makes becomes an extension of oneself, a wish, a prayer, a living joyous experience.

BREAD-BAKING IMPLEMENTS

For bread-baking, it is well to have the following implements on hand: a large, deep bowl with almost vertical sides (3 or 4 quarts or 3 or 4 litres); a small deep bowl; a large wooden working area like a noodle board, about 25 by 18 inches (60 by 45 cm), or a piece of plastic if you prefer it; large glass and metal measuring cups; a nest of measuring spoons; large baking sheets; loaf tins; a rolling pin, the long narrow kind rather than the corn-cob-with-holders type; a dependable oven thermometer; a large sifter; pastry brush; wire rack for cooling; and a strong wooden spoon. A bread hook attachment for heavy-duty mixers is a labour saver. For unusual shapes or for freezing dough: large or small coffee tins with plastic lids; or a child's sand pail of aluminium or unpainted tin. Any shape or form may be practical, *but do not use pans made of galvanized metal;* they are a health hazard as a food container.

Of course, if one is only experimenting and does not plan to bake bread frequently, one can make do with the usual paraphernalia, and use a bed sheet, doubled and thrown over the dining-room table, rather than buying a new board.

BAKING TINS

The shape of bread tins does make a difference to the volume and quality of the loaf of bread. A shallow tin (about 4 by 8½ by 3 inches or 10 by 21 by 7 cm) that holds a 1-lb or a 1½-lb (a 500-g or a 750-g) loaf is preferable to a deep, narrow tin. The loaf bakes more quickly and makes a more attractive slice.

Generally, bakeware should have a dulled or stain-finished interior, though the outside may be polished. Rounded corners are more desirable for ease in removing baked goods and in cleaning.

As to the best kinds of ovenware, a large-scale survey of professional bakers revealed that aluminium was, by far, the preferred metal. Many test kitchens use it as the standard, so that many recipes are temperature-tested in aluminium tins. (This does not mean the tissue-thin, very shiny ones, but good, sturdy, professional-quality tins and never, never scoured with abrasives nor highly polished.) The second preference was high-carbon steel; the third, tin.

Cakes and bread baked in aluminium loaf tins do not develop the crusty sides they will have in the vitreous-enamel pans, that are, on the whole, more popular with home bakers. Ceramic, china and glass types, being good absorbers and heat retainers, require shorter baking periods. They tend, too, to create darker and crustier sides than other materials (25° to 35° F, 10° to 20° C, lower heat than called for in the recipe).

Tinned ware darkens with use and age, causing changes in the baking qualities. This tarnish is a protection and should not be removed with scouring; scraping tends to scratch the surface and make the pan vulnerable to rust. A darker tinned pan will create a darker product than a new polished one, which gives results much like aluminium. Pebbled or waffle-marked surfaces on tinned pans are thought to give better baking results (perhaps to avoid warping), though many experts feel it makes little difference, with which I agree.

For baking sheets, lightweight materials are preferable since they transmit heat rapidly and evenly for quick baking. All thin metal sheets and tins warp if subjected to sudden great changes in temperature, and a warped tin will bake unevenly. Absorption and retention of heat, rather than rapid conduction of heat, is the prime consideration in bakeware. The length of time required for the operation should influence choice of materials: those that are thicker and heavier for foods requiring longer heating time and better heat retention; lightweight materials for short-time use.

SPECIALIZED OVENWARE

Gratin and other baking dishes: Oval, round or square; may be found in copper, steel, aluminium, ceramic, china, glass, etc., and in every size from 4-inch (10-cm) individuals to 14-inch (35-cm) dishes large enough to serve entire families. They do not come with lids.

Moulds: Using a mould is an easy way to transform a mound of everyday food into an appetizing dish attractive enough for a buffet party. The variety of mould shapes and sizes is almost infinite. The most popular materials are copper, aluminium (sometimes with a copper wash) and tinned ware. In Europe, porcelain moulds are very common and vary from elegant and intricate to rustic and simple. Many are ovenproof, but the very thin ones should be used only for jellies, cold salads and desserts. A very thin glass mould for baking has recently been introduced.

Soufflé dishes: With flat bottom, sharply vertical sides and without handles. Traditionally of brown ceramic or white porcelain with a fluted pattern on the outside, though newer ones are available in glass in modern designs.

Casseroles: Whether ceramic (rough or fine, handmade or machine-made), china or porcelain, glass or any metal at all, casseroles are extremely practical and durable if treated with normal care. They have a great variety of uses: for roasting, for pâtés, for the mixtures we call 'casseroles', for rice, polenta or bread puddings, and are often used for serving as well as cooking. Casseroles are available with or without lids, in any shape and depth, sized from tiny individual ramekins to 8- or 10-quart (9½- or 12-litre) capacity. We tend to call many other forms and shapes by the general name of 'casserole', among them terrines (oval or rectangular), *cocottes* and many roasting dishes.

Roasting pans: The large roaster generally used for a turkey or a big roast may also be used for a casserole to serve a large number of people. Aluminium and enamel are the most popular materials. Earthenware roasters are now available in all sizes as are vitreous-enamel roasters (some covered, others not) in a marvellous variety of shapes and colours.

Flan tins and flan dishes: These are round, varying from 6 to 14 inches (15 to 35 cm) in diameter, with a very low rim, often fluted. Detachable bottoms are for ease in cleaning as well as easy removal of the pies. Generally of porcelain, tinned ware, aluminium and sometimes ceramic; they should all be well greased before using.

Tube tins: For angel-food cakes, sponge cakes, etc. These are available also with detachable bottom and tube and an alternative flat bottom; desirable since they serve a number of purposes. Beware of cheap, seamed ones since they permit the batter to run out. Some aluminium ones come with non-stick linings for easy removal. Recently, these types have been suggested for other uses such as meat loaves and pâtés. But if used for angel-food cakes, they should *not be greased.*

Cake tins: There are many variations in sizes and materials: the loaf tin, usually rectangular, and layer tins, commonly round or square. Information on materials is no different from that given for other kinds of tins. The measurements are calculated according to the diameter of the tin rim and many are labelled, with exact sizes, at the factory; the size is either incised on the tin or on an attached label. Use the correct size for each recipe as directed. Cake tins are available with detachable bottoms and clasp-fastened removable sides for easy removal of cakes.

Tools and Implements

With the present increased interest in natural living has come a revival of preoccupation with the old craft of implement-making, and there are now shops selling hand-made wooden spice boxes and chests, small kegs and plant containers. Of course, they are expensive, but lovely.

A good selection of tools in varying sizes is vital to the smooth progress of food preparation, and the availability of these tools can be instrumental in failure or success with a complicated recipe. Some will perform a number of jobs; others will do only one. Some have not changed over the centuries; a few are completely new inventions. Materials, of course, have changed and there have been improvements and many refinements.

KNIVES

While many French cookbooks begin their list of kitchen necessities with the *balance* or scales, most of ours begin with 'a good knife' as the most important of all kitchen tools. Certainly nothing in the kitchen is as potentially dangerous, as time-consuming and as frustrating as a dull knife, or an inadequacy of proper knives. Cuts can be held to a minimum by the use of really sharp knives, a little care and common sense. Although a sharp blade can do more damage to one's fingers than a dull one, the likelihood of cutting oneself in the first place is far less; a sharp blade just doesn't slip as easily. As for the danger to children, knives, like drugs and poisons, should be kept out of their reach, or hidden. Slip old corks over the tips and wrap each separately if kept in a drawer, or hang them high on hooks on the pegboard, or best of all, keep them in a knife case, where the entire blade is protected.

CARE OF KNIVES

A good knife merits good care. I am told that most butchers have professional sharpeners do their knives every week or two, and they will often accommodate customers who bring in their own knives, at very little cost. However, if a tool-sharpening or saw-repair shop is at all convenient, take them there, if you prefer; your knives will then get professional care, and all that's needed between sharpenings is the use of a knife steel or honing steel. It should be remembered that a steel is not meant for sharpening as much as keeping knives sharp and in good shape.

The proper way to use a steel is to hold the steel in the left hand on a slight slant downwards and away from you. Hold the knife in the right hand, sharp blade side towards the steel, and rest the handle end of the knife edge down close to the point of the steel at, say, an angle of twenty degrees. Now draw the knife blade up towards you – from end to point – across the grooved surface of the steel, using only very slight pressure. The steel is held still. Now repeat the action on the other side of the steel with the other edge of the knife. Four or five strokes are usually sufficient.

The other method of manual home-sharpening is with the oil stone. Keep it flat on a firm surface and glide the entire length of the knife blade along the top of the stone, then turn and sharpen the other side. I am not enamoured of electrical sharpening devices for I think they distort the cutting edge, take off too much steel and wear blades down too quickly. Most experts agree.

No knife should be expected to substitute for a jar opener or can opener, or used for cutting string, paper or fabric. Never cut on a hard surface such as glass; always cut on a wood or plastic board.

Do not soak knives or wash them with other articles, greasy or otherwise. Never put them in dishwashers; for even if they have dishwasher-proof handles, it dries them out. The intensely hot water and strong detergent tend to dull both blade and handle. Occasionally, rub the handles with mineral or linseed oil. My carbon-steel knives get discoloured, stained, dirty looking, even, occasionally, if I'm very careless, rusty; but I keep a piece of fine emery cloth (that black sandpaper for metals) under the kitchen sink and a brief rub shines them up in no time; then I wash as usual and dry them promptly. A good-sized old cork dipped in scouring powder and rubbed over the blade will keep blade and fingers functioning properly.

SELECTING KNIVES

The main difference between a good knife and a poor one is its ability to be sharpened properly and to retain that sharpness; an ability that is, in a sense, built into the blade when it is made. Though all knives of the same type look much alike, and all will cut in one way or another, good knives will cut effortlessly and cleanly – and therein lies the difference.

High-carbon steel is generally regarded as the most satisfactory material for knife blades as it takes a sharp edge easily and keeps it for a good long time. Though the edge will need less frequent grinding, the knife requires more care, and if neglected may affect the flavour and colour of some foods. If used to cut such acid foods as citrus fruit or tomatoes, it should be washed and dried immediately after to avoid rust and pitting.

Stainless steel, with chromium replacing the carbon, will not, in general, take or retain as fine an edge, but it is resistant to staining and has no effect on flavour or colour of foods. On the other hand, stainless-steel knives with a high percentage of carbon combine the qualities of the high-carbon and the stainless steels.

Vanadium steel is also a high-carbon steel alloy. It looks much like all stainless steels but it is easy to sharpen, holds its edge as well as high-carbon steel and is extremely tough and durable.

The French produce a most unusual knife that combines carbon steel and *molybdenum*, offering the best qualities of other materials. It will neither dull nor stain.

Another fine quality blade now available is *chrome plated* to make it stainproof, with the high-carbon steel base left exposed on the cutting edge. The plating, like any other, can be scratched and requires great care. Fruit juices and salt may deteriorate the plating, so they should be washed off promptly.

Some knives have *tungsten*, one of the hardest and toughest of all steels, applied to one side of the cutting edge. These must be sharpened by a professional and cannot be done at home. With reasonable care these blades stay sharp for an exceptionally long time. They are, as are all of these last-named exceptional types, very expensive.

The best type of high-carbon steel knife is *hollow-ground steel*, hammer-forged by hand or by machine, to develop a fine grain in the edge. A forged blade will taper gradually from the heel to the point and from the back to the cutting edge. This produces a very practical knife: strong and firm near the handle and flexible near the point.

When selecting a blade be sure it has the proper spring when bent: about one third of the blade from the point should be flexible enough to form a gentle curve, while the other two thirds towards the handle remain rigid. When released, it should spring back to normal position. Should it return very slowly, or remain slightly out of line, you can be sure it will not be very serviceable and may even be made of iron.

The handle and blade should be well balanced to prevent discomfort or strain when used. Handles should feel comfortable in the hand and be easily grasped. The handle should be of moisture- and grease-resistant material. Paint soon flakes and chips or wears off. Impregnated woods are resistant to moisture, grease, heat strain and chipping.

One test of a good-quality knife is the manner in which the handle is attached to the blade. The shank of the knife (that end hidden in the handle) is called the *tang*. In the best knives it extends the full length of the handle and is secured with two or three good-sized rivets. In a cheaply constructed knife, the tang is much shorter and is sometimes simply pushed into the handle and fastened with a small nail or brad and finished with a metal collar where it meets the blade.

TYPES OF KNIVES

A *cleaver* looks somewhat like a cross between a knife and a hatchet. It is very useful in cutting through bones and joints of poultry and meat, for cracking soup bones, for crushing garlic and for cutting lobsters. In Oriental cooking, it is almost indispensable: adventurous cooks wouldn't be without one.

A *paring knife* with a short blade (2½ to 3½ inches, 6 to 8 cm, long) may have a sharp, tapered or blunt point. It is a versatile knife that the homemaker will find constantly in use; apart from paring vegetables and fruits, and slitting meat, it has many other uses.

The *French chef's knife* also has a sturdy blade, anywhere from 8 to 12 inches (20 to 30 cm) long, angled with a raised handle to allow plenty of clearance for knuckles. It is used for dicing and fine chopping (when the tip is held stationary and the cutting is done with a rocking motion). The 8-inch (20-cm) blade is the most practical for general home use.

The *carving knife* has a wide, stiff blade from 9 to 12 inches (23 to 30 cm) long, with a straight back edge, useful for carving roasts.

A *narrow slicer* or ham slicer, with a flexible blade 7 to 10 inches (18 to 25 cm) long, may be used for slicing breads, melons and cold, boneless meats. (A wider, firmer blade is preferred for hot meats.)

The *serrated-edge bread knife* has many uses beside the obvious one; it may be used for cutting cakes and pastries and, when of stainless steel, is ideal for slicing tomatoes and lemons.

These are the most commonly used knives, but there are also grapefruit knives, boning knives, fish scalers and so on, each of which will be found indispensable for its own job.

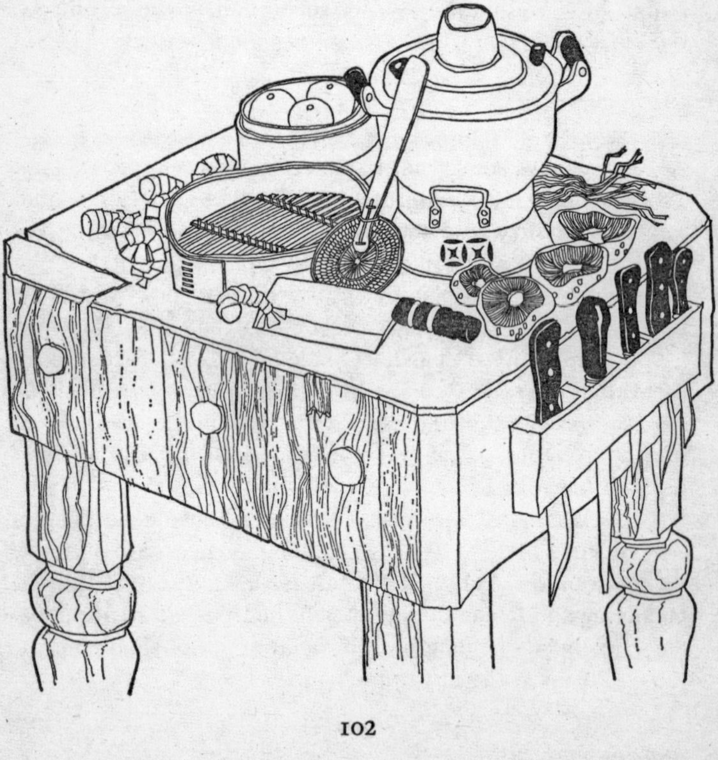

Electric knives are in an entirely different class, since the actual functioning is not motivated by the human hand. There are two blades that work in a reciprocal fashion and cut with a shearing action as one blade meets the other. Cutting is extremely quick and makes even razor-thin slicing easy. Do, by all means, shop around before buying.

WOODEN IMPLEMENTS

Wooden implements are numbered in hundreds. They include salad bowls, chopping bowls with wood-handled, round-edged choppers to fit, bread boards, cutting boards, noodle boards, rolling pins, ravioli pins, meat tenderizers, steak and fish planks, cheese boards, spoons, forks, spatulas, scrapers, butter moulds and paddles, mortars and pestles and many other tools that combine wood and metal such as the indispensable *mandoline* for cutting and slicing vegetables.

Many hold that a wooden implement should never, under any circumstances, be washed. I agree where salad bowls are concerned (unless fish is used in them). When they are only occasionally washed, they tend to get sticky; whereas if never washed but rubbed down with paper towelling after each use and stored in the open air, they remain fresh and well seasoned indefinitely. Should they become stained and too heavily coated, scour them well and sand them down first with coarse and then with fine sandpaper. If they resist this and remain sticky, use denatured alcohol to remove the oil. Then wash with a mild detergent and hot water, wipe with paper towelling, coat with salad oil and store.

A new cutting board should be coated heavily with salad oil and left overnight to 'season'; in the morning, remove all excess oil, and rub with paper towelling until the board looks smooth and dry. This should be done to all wooden boards, no matter what the purpose: work-tops, bread boards, butcher tables, etc.

The best and most serviceable wooden implements used for food preparation are made of hard woods such as cherry, beech, boxwood, certain oaks and rock maple. It should be unpainted, very smoothly surfaced raw wood or finished with a penetrating wood sealer. When treated in this way, implements rarely need more than a brisk rub with paper towelling, although the use of warm water or a damp cloth is occasionally necessary and good for the wood. On the other hand, prolonged soaking, use of strong detergents and abrasives, or over-zealous drying close to heat are guaranteed to cause splitting, warping and drying out of the natural oils. Never wash wooden implements in the dishwasher. Never let them soak in the general dishwater.

Bread boards sometimes acquire a slightly mouldy odour if kept in a closed place. Sprinkle with salt and rub with a cut lemon half. (This will also prevent darkening.) Wash as usual and dry out in the sun, if possible, but never near a hot stove or source of central heating.

Those implements that are combined with metal, like hand-choppers and vegetable-slicers, should be cleaned promptly after use and well dried. They may be oiled to prevent rust and stored in an airy, dry place.

A cautionary note: It has been found that cutting boards used for both raw meats and for foods not meant to be

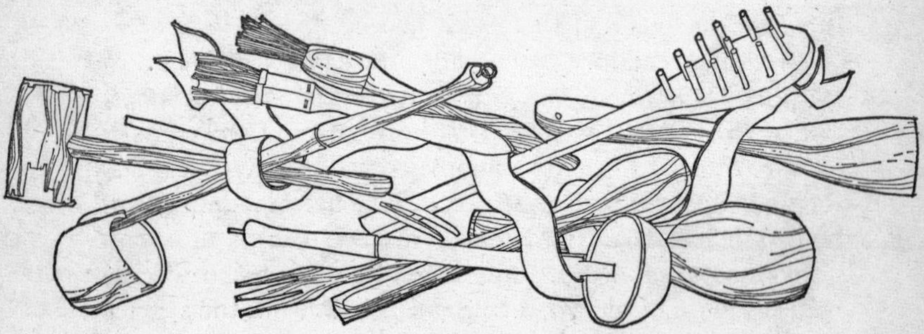

cooked (salad greens, etc.) can become a breeding ground for Salmonella, which in large numbers causes a very serious type of food poisoning. Thorough cooking destroys it, but if spread to uncooked foods it can cause intense suffering. Contaminated areas, if allowed to stand at temperatures between 45° and 140°F (7° and 60°C), are perfect breeding grounds. It has been advised that two boards be used, one for raw meats and poultry, and the other for foods to be eaten raw. To treat a cutting board, home economists suggest that a solution of 1 tablespoonful of chlorine bleach (laundry bleach) per quart (or litre) of cold water be poured over the board; rinse well under very hot running water and wipe with paper towelling. Dry very slowly, out in the sun, if possible.

If wooden bowls, boards or other implements become chipped or cracked, they may be unsanitary and indeed hazardous to use. Discard or refinish the article: remove the old finish with sandpaper, first coarse, then fine. Mix 1 tablespoonful of mineral oil with powdered pumice stone and rub well into the inside of the vessel with cheesecloth or paper towelling until the wood feels dry and smooth (about half an hour). Leave to dry for twenty-four hours. Remove the pumice dust and repeat the process. You may have to do this a few times before you are satisfied. Then wash the implement in the usual way and proceed to use.

OTHER IMPLEMENTS

Kitchen shears and *poultry shears* are invaluable aids in protecting your knives. They have many uses: to cut up poultry, to trim fish, to chop up herbs and green onions. As the handles are formed to act as a number of other useful tools, they can be used to pry up jar lids, to act as small pliers, bottle openers and so on.

Spatulas are most convenient when of a stain-resistant material with perfectly straight sides. One of their most popular uses is for levelling off dry ingredients in measuring cups and spoons. They should be flexible at the ends and rigid towards the handle in order to lift foods better. They are available in various sizes and types to fit particular needs.

Work forks are, like knives, of various types, having from two to four tines. Handles should have the same characteristics as knife handles and be firmly attached.

Work spoons are available with slotted openings, round openings and solid. Stainless-steel ones with long handles are most practical. A good variety is essential in all kitchens for skimming, stirring, lifting, draining and even beating. Wooden spoons are of course a *must* if you value your pots and pans. If you do not like wood, however, the nylon ones are more resistant to stain and wear.

Scrapers are about as necessary as knives and indeed are indispensable when using blenders and for the complete removal of food from bowls, containers and pans. They are available in plastic or in rubber, moulded in one piece or with detachable handles. The scraper should be washed immediately after use, especially after use on fatty foods, for fats tend to cause rubber to deteriorate.

Plastic chopping/slicing boards are now generally available, and for those housekeepers who are too lax to sterilize wooden boards properly, this is the ideal implement: it will not absorb grease, odours or germs; it is lightweight and easily moved around; it is simple to clean; it is soft enough

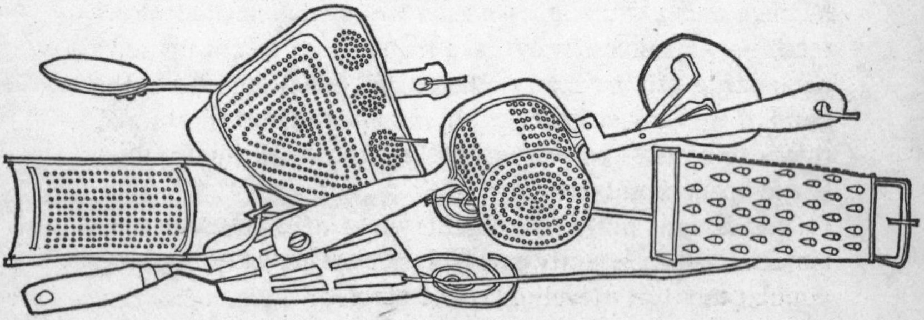

not to dull fine knives. A Japanese friend who has been using hers for over four years said, 'I do not know whether it dulls knives or not; I keep my honing stone near by and simply rub the knife over it three or four times before slicing, so it's always sharp.' The perfect housekeeper.

A *French frying basket* may come with a saucepan or without, and is a must for those who do any deep frying at all. This is a much more convenient method than frying in a skillet, once one grows accustomed to it, for it leaves the food less oily, and there is no danger of food or batter sticking to a pan. It may be used to fry or boil potatoes, corn-on-the-cob, eggs, fish, vegetables, fried breads and pastries ... over oil or water.

A *heat distributor* is indispensable for those who are rushed or watching a number of pans at the same time. This device creates an air space below the pan to keep it from direct heat. It is an alternative to the old-fashioned (but still effective) asbestos pad.

MORTAR AND PESTLE, BLENDER AND MINCER

The mortar and pestle is probably one of the most unchanged of all objects. Once the habit of using it is acquired, it becomes as indispensable as a work spoon or a knife. The modern blender has superseded it in many ways for many tasks, but there are some jobs that cannot be done as well in the blender, for it does its job too well. The mincer (or meat mincer) has also taken over some of the tasks once done only with the mortar and pestle, but it, too, is not the same thing. When, for example, grinding up herbs and spices, a bronze mortar and pestle will do the job with a kind of unevenness that the other implements cannot duplicate. It is the kind of unevenness that leaves a certain margin for flavour reminiscent of European country cooking, which cannot be achieved with a machine.

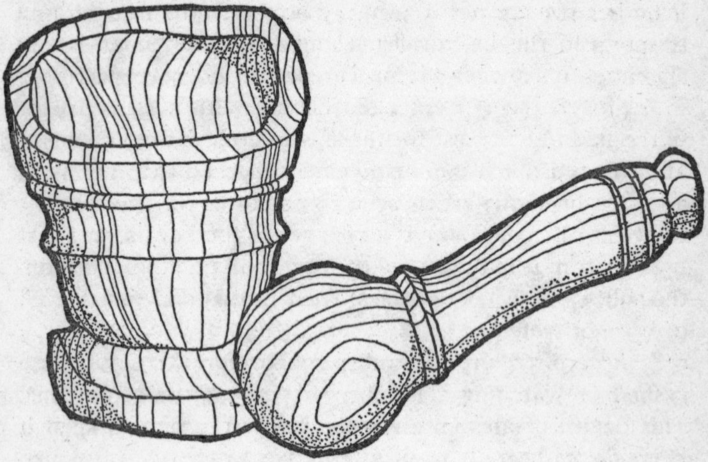

In my childhood memories, one of the most achingly beautiful objects in my mother's kitchen was the bronze mortar and pestle that her mother had brought from Russia in 1906 (with the copper kettle). As a child I can remember begging for the pleasure of polishing it! Imagine! It is now in my kitchen. I use it often and still polish it with great pleasure.

I also have a tiny bisque one of unglazed porcelain (from France) for mashing a single clove of garlic with other herbs and spices; a rough Mexican one for spices like cloves that are too hard to do well in other materials; and a small bronze one (from Florence) for more general needs. To start up a large blender for such small amounts is impractical. Besides, one wants the garlic ground up, not liquefied. At least, I do. Another thing to be said for a mortar and pestle, whatever the size or material: it is probably the most attractive ornament for any kitchen of whatever style.

SCALES

Whether you are one of those cooks who weigh everything or one who weighs almost nothing, you will find that there are times when kitchen scales are essential. When choosing the right scales for your needs there are a number of points to consider. You must first decide what size scales you want. This depends partly on how much space you have in your kitchen and partly on the quantities you are likely to want to weigh. If you have a very small kitchen you will not want enormous scales that take up half of your work-top or shelf space, but you may find scales that can be attached to the wall very useful. You must also decide whether you are likely to need scales with a capacity of 5, 10 or 30 pounds (2½, 5 or 10 kilos).

All scales come with detachable containers into which you put the item to be weighed. Choose the shape of container that will best suit your purpose – they can be round bowls, flat trays or triangular dishes – and decide whether you prefer plastic, which is easy to clean, or sturdier material.

Scales can be spring-balanced, beam or sliding weight scales, or counter scales. With the spring-balance type, the item to be weighed presses on a spring which makes a pointer move round a dial or along a scale. With the beam scales, you slide weights along the pivoted beams on the front of the scales until they counter-balance the weight in the pan. With either of these types you should be able to zero the scales when necessary. Make sure they are easy to adjust. The traditional counter scales have a set of loose weights which you put on one side of the scales to balance the item to be weighed on the other side. These are the loveliest scales and if you can afford the decorative old pieces with bronze and marble, and handsome weights stored in a pretty wooden box, so much the better.

Most of the reputable makes are reasonably accurate, but it is a good idea to test for accuracy as soon as you can so

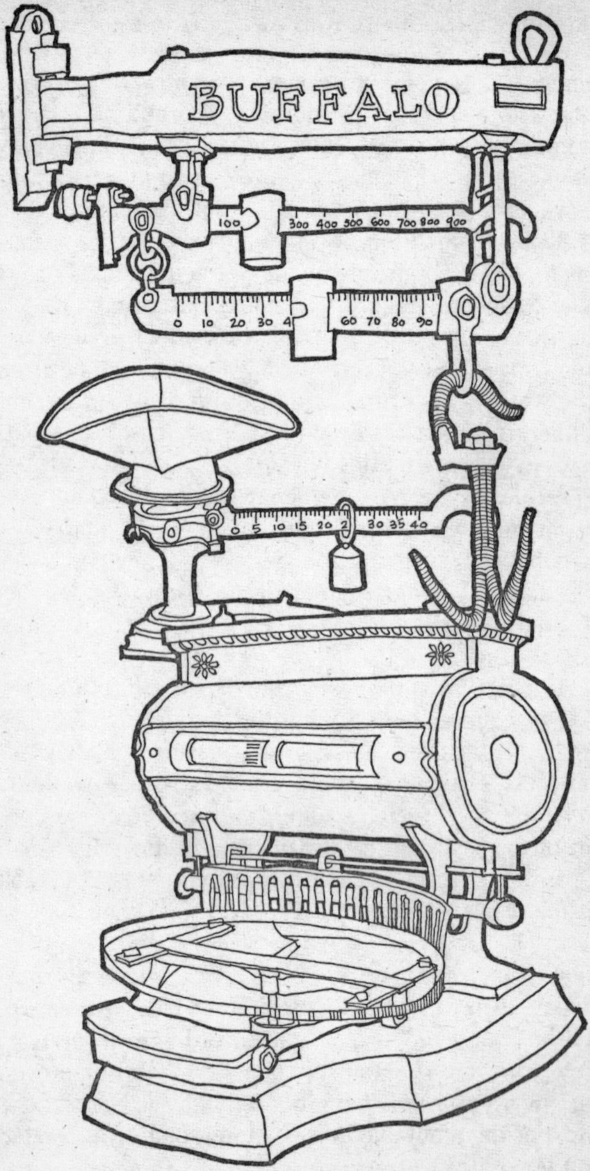
BUFFALO
100
300 400 500 600 700 800 900
0 10 20 30 4
60 70 80 90
0 5 10 15 20 2
30 35 40

that you can return the scales if you are not satisfied. Of course, great accuracy is more essential when you are weighing small amounts than when you are weighing several pounds or kilos.

Whatever kinds of scales you choose, make sure that you can read them easily. Some have dials which look extremely confusing and some have markings at an awkward level so you have to crane your neck to decipher them.

With the advent of metrication it is now more or less essential to have scales that give both metric and imperial measurements. Most of those available now do give both, but you may not find beam scales that give the two systems.

One last point about choosing scales: for very small quantities (of less than 1 ounce or 25 or 30 grams) it is often easier to use spoons than to weigh ingredients, and recipes often give small amounts in terms of teaspoons, etc., but if you find you do often need to weigh such quantities you should find a scale that has divisions smaller than 1 ounce or 25 grams in the first section of its range, or buy a separate scale for very small amounts.

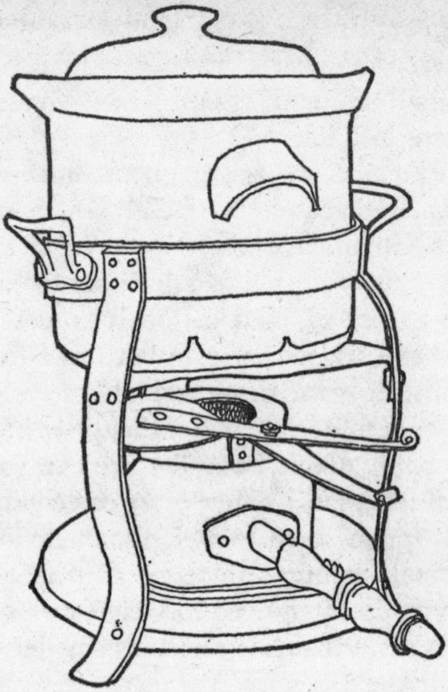

Exotica

In shopping for kitchenware, the homemaker soon realizes that more and more equipment of the type once only made abroad is now being made domestically, and in a great variety of materials and prices. In buying unusual and interesting objects of kitchen equipment, the rules set down in former chapters should guide your judgement. The price of an article does not necessarily indicate its quality but, on the whole, a heavy, well-made and well-balanced item will cost more than a carelessly made one, though other factors must be considered: an unusual design, an unusual combination of materials and the type of shop in which one makes the selection, among them.

Objects of particular interest, such as a wok or a couscous steamer, a paella pan or a polenta pot, may possibly be less expensive if bought in a shop specializing in foods and equipment of an ethnic group and located in the neighbourhood in which that ethnic group is gathered, rather than in an elegant shop devoted to all kinds of kitchen equipment. This is not always true, but often enough to make it worth the try.

Those who have tasted exotic culinary delights in foreign lands, and wish to reproduce them at home as they are cooked and served in their original *milieux*, will be interested in the descriptions that follow. I have chosen these particular vessels as they are available now in many of the larger kitchen equipment shops as well as in foreign quarters of large cities. Alternatively, they can be ordered for you.

I also feel that these utensils make for unusual entertaining.

The recipes for dishes used in these utensils are not difficult to locate, on the whole. Almost any large library will have books devoted to general international cuisine or specializing in the cuisine of one country. Recipes for *garbures* and pâtés, the Italian chicken roasted in a terracotta vessel, Japanese tempura, any number of Chinese dishes for use in the wok, are often included with the utensil.

The *Chinese wok*: Orientals prefer to spend much more time on preparation than on actual cooking. Most recipes demand more vegetables than meat or fish, and they are sliced, diced or finely chopped so that they may cook rapidly in very little liquid. Of course, all ingredients are prepared in advance and arranged in small bowls near at hand. Cooking oil, thickening agents and seasonings are also conveniently close. All must be ready before the cooking starts. One cannot stop to search out a forgotten item and to pare it once the process has begun. Hard, fast cooking is one of the secrets of good Oriental cookery. That is, foods are cooked just enough to sterilize but not to destroy flavour, colour, texture or nutrients. Thus, having the proper equipment is vital.

The wok is the main utensil used. It is a wide, round pot like a shallow hemisphere with handles on opposite sides up close to the rim or with one wooden handle. It usually sits on a metal collar, raised above high heat. This kind of cooking is called by the Chinese 'stir-frying'. The cook, using shovel-like implements, moves the food constantly, from the bottom up along the sides, around, under, lifting and tossing steadily. In the Orient this is done over a charcoal fire; in this country it is done best over a gas flame. But you may recall that a round-bottomed pan leaves much to be desired on an electric burner, so there is now a modified wok with bottom lopped off and left nicely flat. In the hardware shops of Chinatown, one may find woks in gleaming stainless steel and even some with copper bottoms. Obviously, iron is the ideal metal for hard, fast cooking, so most woks are constructed of sheet or drawn steel and must be 'seasoned' in the usual way (see sections on seasoning iron and steel utensils, pages 52–3 and 57). If, during your initial effort with the wok, your food should burn and stick, the pan must be re-seasoned.

A visit to any good kitchenware shop should yield many other titillating finds, among them other implements and tools for use with the wok: a lid and long-handled turners, ladles and strainers, stacked steaming baskets, and so on. Get a package of chopsticks and learn to use them deftly; they are a great convenience in setting pieces of food into the wok and lifting them out. The Chinese cleaver is a most versatile and beautiful instrument, and nothing will work as well for crushing a piece of garlic, cutting bony meats and poultry, chopping, even slicing when you get clever enough.

The *paella pan* is a Spanish invention, not unlike a modified wok: a flat bottom slopes gently up to the rim with handles opposite each other along the edge. Like the wok, it is usually constructed of sheet or drawn steel and must be seasoned. Paella is a rice dish composed of small pieces of food: fish, shellfish, chicken or rabbit, veal and many kinds of vegetables. It is a traditional dish and there are as many versions as there are of gazpacho, and that is infinite. It can go into the oven and does require much longer cooking that most Chinese dishes, but is at its best when cooked fairly rapidly.

The *French wire fish grill* looks not unlike a simple piece of modern sculpture. Even if never used for cooking, it is still a lovely piece of decoration for kitchen or dining room. About 16 inches (40 cm) long, it encages the entire fish for grilling over charcoal and has legs for raising it above the heat.

Rosette irons are used for preparing a type of thin batter-fried cake. The irons come in many shapes: flowers, butterflies or simple roses. An iron is composed of an openwork, cast-metal head with a long handle. The head is dipped into the batter and then into the deep fat, which should be hot enough to cook the 'cake' rapidly. It is served with fine sugar or maple sugar. In any case, the irons are lovely, airy objects.

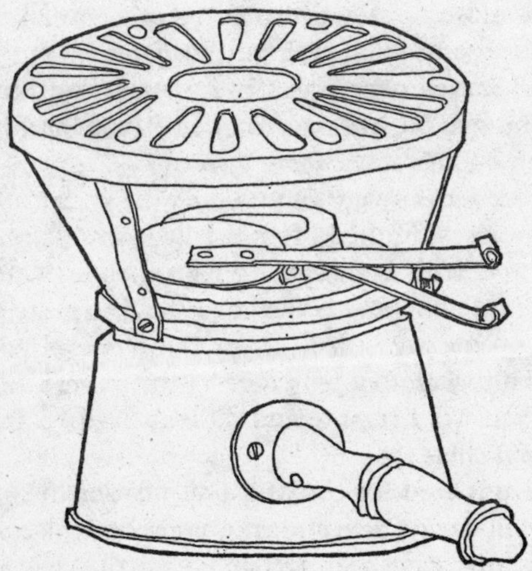

The *egg-white beating bowl* is the large, hemispherical, unlined copper bowl that is never used over heat, but only for beating up egg whites. It is described more fully in the section on copper. With it, one should have a large wire balloon whisk.

The *sabayon bowl* is much like the egg-white one, but has a handle and is much smaller. It is, of course, used over heat to make this absolutely delectable dessert, the recipe for which is included in many general cookbooks, as well as in Italian ones. Both the sabayon and egg-white bowls should be of heavy copper, or just don't bother unless you plan to use them only for decoration.

The *Italian polenta pot* is usually of hand-hammered heavy copper, unlined, and is, by our definition, a kettle, having a bail handle by which it is hung over a fire. The bottom is slightly rounded and it will work well over a gas flame, but not too well over an electric unit. I find that it helps a little to use a wire grid, of the type employed with flameproof glass, to make some basic connection. But this is one pot that requires constant attention. In Italy, polenta (a kind of cornmeal porridge) is used as a substitute for pasta, and most pasta sauces can be used over polenta. In the north, an autumnal dish is tiny game birds roasted or grilled and served over polenta. An American polenta pot now on the market has one wooden handle and resembles an overturned high hat.

A *salamander* is a very old tool; its use goes back beyond the Middle Ages. Named after the little fire animal, it is a long iron rod with a flattened widened end. Heated in the fire until white hot, it is waved over food to glaze or brown it, much as we put a dish under the flame briefly. Sometimes it is dipped into a punch or 'glogg' to heat it. It is used today only in very remote and rather primitive areas or by professional chefs.

A *tripière* is used for cooking a dish native to Normandy, *tripes à la mode de Caen*, and enormously popular in France. It is a ceramic casserole, rather flatter than usual and of medium size, with a lid that fits down into the pot and leaves a flat surface on the top.

The *Mongolian huo kuo* is a tin-lined brass utensil, of two parts, traditionally used for the 'chrysanthemum pot' (related to the *fondue bourguignonne*). Small pieces of food are cooked in a stock in the upper part of this pot, which fits over a charcoal fire in the lower pot. There is a chimney in the centre. It is a marvellous and amusing item for the congenial, casual cocktail party. It is also called *chrysanthemum pot* or *Mongolian hot pot*.

The *toupin* is the proper pot for cooking and serving the

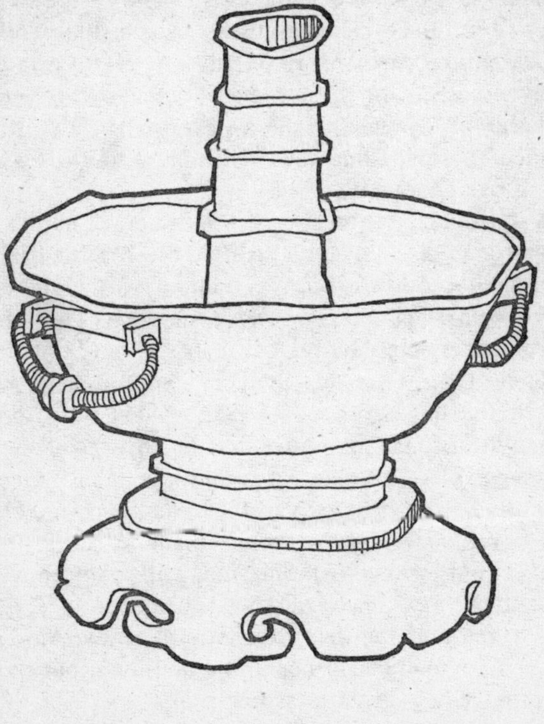

Basque dish called a *garbure*. It is a little earthenware pot, delightfully shaped with a chubby contour, a round bottom and a long neck. On each side there are round handles and a stick-out handle juts out between them on one side. The lid fits deeply and the edge comes out beyond the pot rim. *Garbure* is a soup: thick, delicious and filling, using beans, cabbage, turnips, potatoes, ham hocks, cheese and croûtons – an entire meal.

French pâté moulds and terrines vary enough to accommodate any requirements in material as well as quantity and type of pâté to be made. The tin moulds that come apart are for pâté en croûte (encased in a pastry crust) and result in a very decorative product. The porcelain terrines are sometimes glazed on the outside with an earthy look and the lid sports the head of a duck or rabbit; or they may be entirely of white porcelain and very businesslike. There are also clear-glazed earthenware terrines, oval or rectangular. All have close-fitting lids, a requirement of the recipe. Terrines are now available almost everywhere that kitchen equipment is sold. I find them extremely useful for many forms of oven cookery.

The *couscoussière* (or couscous steamer) is used for the North African dish called couscous; a more delightful party dish I do not know. The pot is actually a steamer, composed of two round-sided pots, one above the other. The couscous is a product of semolina related to pasta, but consisting of tiny uneven pieces, made by being rubbed between the palms of the hands instead of being rolled out. Couscous has many versions. Sometimes the broth is made with as many vegetables and kinds of meat as possible; sometimes it is simply made with few vegetables and one kind of meat or fowl. Whichever way, broth is made in the lower pot; the upper pot, which is perforated, is lined with a damp towel and the moistened couscous is placed in it. The pot is then covered and the dish steams until ready. Most couscoussières are made of rather thin aluminium, but they are also available now in stainless steel.

The *fish kettle* is designed for poaching an entire fish. It is a long, narrow, two-handled pot, containing a rack with high, vertical handles, used for lifting, as the fish rests on the rack. It is a typically French utensil, infrequently used and usually very expensive, even in aluminium or tinned steel. In copper it is stunning, but the price! However, once bought, it should last for a few generations. No one in the world could call it a basic piece of equipment, but it is a coveted treasure for the serious cook.

Omelette pans are becoming extremely popular and are now quite easy to find. They should be of a heavy metal; traditionally of carbon steel. The most practical sizes are 8 or 10 inch (20 to 25 cm) with sloping sides so the omelette may slide easily out of the pan. Be sure to use the balance test (page 83), for an unbalanced omelette pan may easily spell disaster. Another omelette pan is a two-sided one,

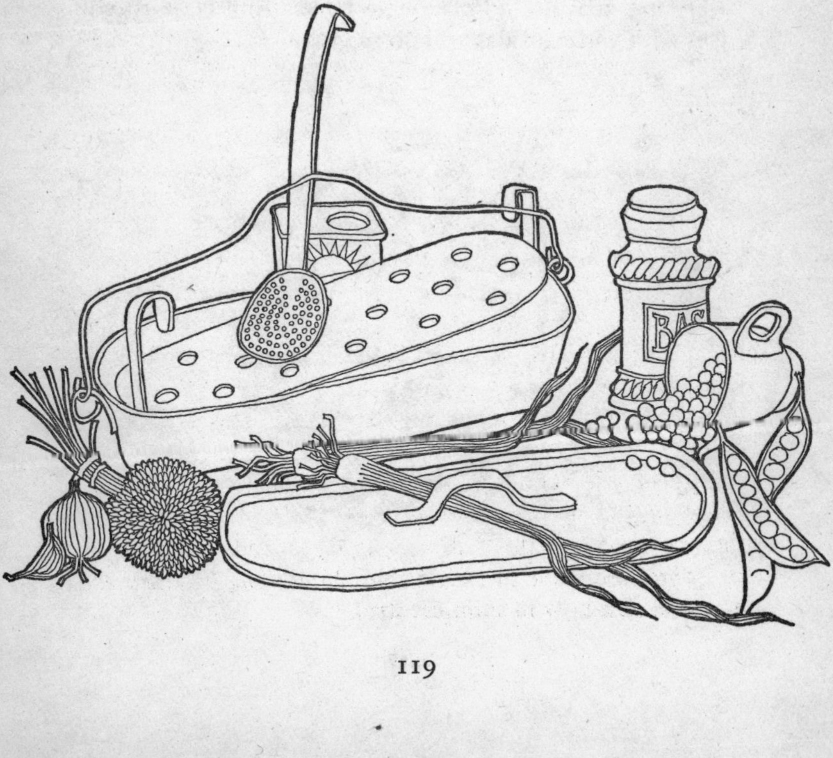

joined by a hinge; each side has its own handle. The purpose is to be able to fold the omelette by lifting one side and setting it on the other. These are often made of aluminium; be sure it is thick enough to prevent burning.

Crêpe pans, blini pans, oval fish or trout pans are all variations of the frying-pan, and they vary according to the practical aspects of their uses. A steel crêpe pan is more practical, and much cheaper, than a copper one. Even professional chefs use steel except for show-off times when the entire dish is made before a customer. Blinis are the Russian type of crêpe, and the blini pan is usually smaller with sides that are rounded and more vertical than those of the crêpe pan, which flare outwards. The oval trout pan is distinguished by a long handle that shoots out from the wide instead of the narrow side of the oval.

A *bain-marie* is merely a large shallow pan to be filled with hot water in which pans and pots are set for even warming. It is a kind of double boiler. Any large roasting pan with vertical sides will do the job.

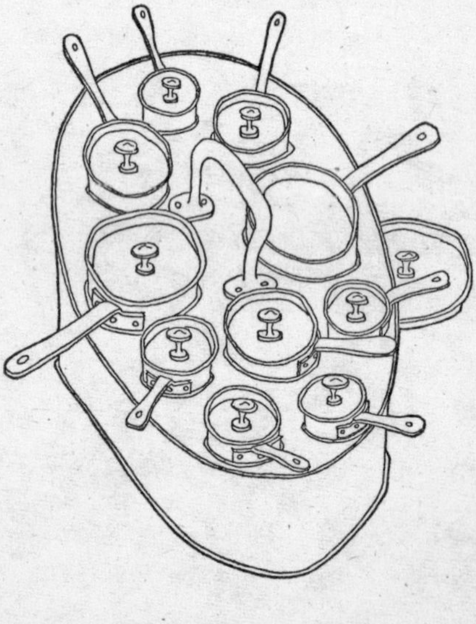

Basics

This list of basic needs for a small kitchen, serving two or three persons, should take care of all immediate requirements. To it can be added whatever other exotic and amusing implements one will want with the gaining of experience and the widening of tastes. Do not buy pans larger than needed. Perhaps it is done in a spirit of economy, with the thought that a larger pot will serve many purposes. A larger pot than is needed encourages the cooking of more food and using more fuel than necessary. A large pot containing a small amount of food is more liable to burn. A large pot also requires large storage space.

1-quart (1-litre) saucepan, with cover
1½-quart (2-litre) saucepan, with cover
3-quart (3½-litre) saucepan, with cover
(If these have detachable or heat-proof handles, they will serve the double purpose of acting as casseroles for oven cookery. Or if one of the last two is chosen with low sides, it will serve for poaching eggs, heating frozen vegetables or small amounts of stews.)
3 frying-pans or skillets (4-inch, 8-inch and 12-inch; or 10-cm, 20-cm and 30-cm)
A large casserole with cover for parties
2 coffee pots (2-cup and 8-cup)
Tea kettle (2- or 3-quart; or 2½- to 3½-litre)
1½-quart (2-litre) double boiler
Roasting pan, with rack
10-inch (25-cm) pie plate (can be used for baking other things)
3-piece mixing-bowl set
Large colander
2 strainers, different sizes, *plus* a
Conical vegetable strainer with wooden forcer, called a *chinois*
Lettuce basket (learn to use one; you will never be sorry)
1 set of implements composed of: 1 solid spoon, 1 slotted spoon, 1 long-handled fork, 1 spatula, 1 ladle, 1 potato masher and whatever else you fancy

Variety of wooden implements: 2 long-handled spoons, 2 short-handled spoons, 1 slotted spoon, 1 egg spoon (for lifting out boiled eggs, it has a round hole)
Chopping board (12 to 14 inches, or 30 to 35 cm, at least)
Wire whisk (for egg whites, whipped cream or mayonnaise)
Rotary egg-beater
4-sided grater with varying slots
Vegetable steaming rack, collapsible
2 funnels, varying sizes
Flour sifter
Heat distributor
Knives (page 96)
Vegetable slicer or *mandoline*
Vegetable peeler
Egg slicer (also for tomatoes and mushrooms)
Food mincer
Corkscrew
Measuring cups and spoons

OPTIONALS

Exotics: omelette pan, wok, paella pan and all the other desirables listed in the last section
Baking tins: these are listed in the section devoted to baking (page 92)
Dessert moulds
Set of skewers of varying sizes
Pressure cooker
French frying basket
Hot-pot trivets
Kitchen tongs
Cheesecloth
Tape measure
Scallop shells for elegant serving
Scales

Terminology

Acrylic: A synthetic substance, rarely used on cookware, that is painted on to the base metal and baked at a very high temperature. Safe for normal kitchen use, it is often found on bread boxes, canisters, metal cabinets, etc.

Anodizing: Produced by an electrolytic process that coats aluminium with a tough, wear-resistant (oxide) surface. Recommended particularly for bakeware, it will speed up baking periods by as much as 30 per cent. Some articles are coloured, but these cannot be used in dishwashers and should not, in any case, have prolonged contact with liquids as they fade easily. Sometimes used on lids of surface cookware.

Cast metal (aluminium or iron): Produced by pouring molten metal into a heavy steel mould; results in durable, heavy utensils completely without seams.

Ceramic or earthenware: Clay, fired at a very high temperature to hardness. Generally recommended for ovenware.

Ceramic coating: An interior and/or exterior glass-like finish, fused to the base metal. It will not easily scratch or mark; nor is the colour affected by normal wear or dishwasher cleaning. Generally an interchangeable term for porcelain coating or enamelware.

Drawn aluminium or pressed aluminium: Made by rolling heavy-gauge sheets under intense pressure, then stretching into the desired shape. The rolling process increases the density and durability of the metal and makes it uniform in thickness.

Enamelware: Another term for ceramic or porcelain coating.

Galvanized metal: See Zinc.

Gauge: The term used to indicate the thickness of a metal as measured in thousandths of an inch. Thicker metals have lower gauge numbers (i.e., a light utensil of 22 gauge is .25 of an inch (6.25 mm) thick; a heavy utensil of 12 gauge is .80 of an inch (2 cm) thick). The thicker the utensil, the stronger and more resistant to dents and warping, and the more expensive.

Plating: A coating of metal fused to the surface of another metal, usually by an electroplating process, such as silver plating.

Polyamide finish: Looks much like porcelain or enamel, but is a synthetic of the nylon family, like acrylic, though stronger.

It is said to be unaffected by any substance in kitchen use. Sometimes called 'baked enamel' or by various trade names.

Porcelain: A form of clayware, usually white, very fine and dense.

Porcelain finish: A term interchangeable with ceramic finish.

Satin finish: A dull finish applied to certain bright smooth metals to improve heat conduction.

Spinning or spun metal (steel or aluminium): Made by fastening the blank sheet of metal to the rounded side of a mould which is then spun or rotated as the metal is shaped over it. Usually used only for objects which will not be subjected to great strain or changes in temperature.

Stainless steel: A steel or iron alloy which must contain at least 11½ per cent of chromium. Finer qualities also contain nickel.

Stamped utensils: Made from a sheet of cold, thin metal put through a stamping machine. As the metal is very thin, and may even be brittle, they bend, break and warp easily.

Terracotta: Unglazed ceramic.

Tinware or tinned steel: Steel or iron coated with shiny tin.

Weight: Not necessarily synonymous with strength. A light utensil may be durable and tough; a heavy one may well be fragile or made of inferior materials in an inferior way.

Zinc: A coating to protect the base metal from rust (also called galvanized iron or galvanized steel). Never used for food containers and considered hazardous for cooking or holding food.

Index